Judaism in th

ISSUES IN RELIGIOUS STUDIES

Professor Peter Baelz and Jean Holm

Also available in this series
Interpreting Religious Experience, Peter Donovan
Evil, Suffering and Religion, Brian Hebblethwaite

Judaism in the First Century

HYAM MACCOBY

SHELDON PRESS
LONDON

First published in Great Britain in 1989 by
Sheldon Press, Marylebone Road, London NW1 4DU

British Library Cataloguing in Publication Data
Maccoby, Hyam
  Judaism in the first century.
  1. Judaism, 1–70
  I. Title
  296'.09'01

  ISBN 0–85969–550–6

Typeset by J&L Composition Ltd, Filey, N. Yorkshire
Printed in Great Britain by Biddles Ltd, Guildford, Surrey

General Preface to the Series

This series of books offers an introduction to some of the central issues involved in religious studies. It aims to be as dispassionate as possible, assuming a serious interest on the part of the reader but neither previous study in the area nor commitment to any religious position. It seeks to combine a basic rigour of thought with a concreteness of approach.

The purpose of each book is to indicate the nature of the issue, the questions raised by it, and the main directions in which thinkers have looked for answers to such questions. It should thus provide a firm foundation on which further study can be built.

The series was designed in the first place to meet the needs of students embarking on courses in religious studies in colleges of education and universities, and of senior pupils following the revised 'A' level syllabuses. However, the books are not in any narrow sense 'text books', and it is hoped that they will be of value to anyone approaching a study of these issues for the first time.

Peter Baelz and Jean Holm

*In loving memory of
Zipporah Maccoby,
my mother*

Contents

1

Pharisees and Sadducees

Most people's notions of first-century Judaism are derived from the New Testament. From this source they gather that the leading religious group among the Jews was called 'the Pharisees', but that there was also another group called the Sadducees, whose views differed in some respects from those of the Pharisees. A close reading of the New Testament would reveal the fact that the High Priest was a Sadducee (Acts 5.17); but there is little or nothing there to suggest that there were such important differences between the Pharisees and the Sadducees that the High Priest was not regarded by the Pharisees as speaking for them on religious matters at all. Yet this is in fact the case (see chapter 2). This is an instance of the important point that the New Testament is not a wholly reliable source of information about the Jewish religious scene. It gives a hostile and undiscriminating picture of Jewish religion during our period, though this does not mean that its evidence is valueless. When one allows for its bias, there is much of historical value to be learnt from it.

For our main information about first-century Judaism, however, we must turn to other sources: to the inter-Testamental literature, especially the Pseudepigrapha (see chapter 2) to the recently discovered Dead Sea Scrolls; to the writings of the historian Josephus and the philosopher Philo; and, above all, to the rabbinic writings, which throw a flood of light on the religious attitudes of the Pharisees and their successors, the Rabbis. Particularly valuable for our period are the rabbinic liturgy and the Targums (see chapter 6), though the Tannaitic literature (Mishnah, Tosefta, Mekilta, Sifra, Sifre) and the later Talmuds and Midrashim also contain much relevant material.

Modern scholars, making use of all these sources, have been able to build up a much more authentic and sympathetic picture of first-century Judaism than was previously available. The new impression that has emerged is one of vitality and richness of variety. It seems that Judaism, in the first century, was in a very creative phase. Sects and movements proliferated, each trying to solve the religious problems that were so pressing: what was the Jewish role in the era of Roman power? How could the visions and promises of the Hebrew Bible be made relevant in the hard conditions of subjection? Christianity (in its earliest phase a Jewish sect) was only one of these responses to the problems set by the period. The discovery of the Dead Sea Scrolls has given us understanding of one hitherto unknown, or imperfectly known, sect, and the likelihood is now accepted that there were many more, not included in the traditional list; consequently, the Apocryphal and Pseudepigraphic literature is now regarded as stemming from a multitude of sects.

Nevertheless, the evidence from both Josephus and the New Testament, as also from the rabbinic literature, is that the two most prominent movements were the Pharisees and the Sadducees. It makes a good starting-point, therefore, to consider the major characteristics of these two movements, and how they differ from each other. Such consideration will bring out the main religious dilemmas of the period, common to all Jewish groups; and also enable us to correct some popular misconceptions that stand in the way of understanding first-century Judaism, particularly the idea that Pharisaism represents a phase of stagnation in Jewish history.

The Oral Torah

The chief doctrinal point at issue between the Pharisees and the Sadducees was over what was called 'the Oral Torah'; but this was a point of difference which had enormous consequences for their respective religious, political and institutional outlooks. The word '*Torah*' (often mistranslated as 'Law') means 'Teaching'. Both Pharisees and Sadducees accepted the validity of the Written Torah, comprising the books of the Hebrew Bible. The most authoritative part was the Pentateuch, the Five Books of Moses, containing the details of the revelation given to Moses on Mount Sinai, with which Judaism as a religion began. But the Pharisees also believed that there was another source of religious teaching called the Oral Torah, comprising traditions that had been handed down to accompany and explain the words of the Written Torah. Moreover, they believed that the Oral Torah was not a static body of knowledge, but was continually developing and growing, as new additions were made to it by each generation, applying the eternal principles of the Written Torah to new problems and the conditions of their own times.

The Sadducees, on the other hand, rejected these extra-biblical developments, declaring that all necessary truths were to be found in the Bible itself.

This basic difference between the Pharisees and the Sadducees is expressed by Josephus (the Jewish historian of these times, who wrote about 90 C.E.) as follows:

> ... the Pharisees have delivered to the people a great many observances by succession from their fathers, which are not written in the laws of Moses: and for that reason it is that the Sadducees reject them, and say that we are to esteem those observances to be obligatory which are in the written word, but are not to observe what are derived from the tradition of our forefathers

(*Antiquities* XIII. 10.6(293))

In the same passage, Josephus makes it clear that the Pharisees were not merely transmitters of traditions, but were themselves active legislators, and that the Sadducees wished to 'abolish the decrees' of the Pharisees. That the Pharisees were both transmitters of traditions and creative legislators is amply confirmed in the rabbinic writings, which record both processes in great detail.

How did these two religious movements arise among the Jews? It seems clear that they arose in response to a very important religious event: the completion of the canon of the Hebrew Bible (called by Christians the 'Old Testament').

The Hebrew Bible was divided into three sections:

(1) the Pentateuch, to which alone the name 'Torah' properly belonged, though sometimes this name was extended to the whole Hebrew Bible;

(2) the Prophets (Hebrew, *Nebi'im*): these included not only the books of the literary prophets, Isaiah, Jeremiah, Ezekiel and the twelve 'minor' prophets, but also the historical works, Joshua, Judges, Samuel and Kings (but not Chronicles). These historical works were considered to have been written with full prophetic inspiration;

(3) the Writings (Hebrew, *Ketubim*): these were works considered to have been written 'through the Holy Spirit', but not with full prophetic power. Included among these were the book of Daniel, the Psalms, Proverbs and Chronicles.

This threefold division gave rise to the Jewish name for the 'Bible', which is *Tanakh*. This is formed from the initial letters of *Torah, Nebi'im* and *Ketubim*.

Thus the order of the Hebrew Bible is not the same as that found in Christian editions of the 'Old Testament', in which a scheme derived from the Greek Septuagint is followed, based more on literary genres than on the degree of inspiration assigned.

Both Pharisees and Sadducees agreed that the canon was now complete, in the sense that no more books, as yet unwritten, would be added to it. There continued to be some argument about whether certain books, already written, should be included in the canon, particularly the Wisdom of Ben Sira (Ecclesiasticus), Ecclesiastes and the Song of Songs.

Another way of putting this is that both parties agreed that 'inspiration had ceased', but this is a negative way of regarding the matter. A better way is to say that the two parties disagreed about the meaning of the concept of 'revelation'.

The Sadducees thought that God had given his revelation in the written form of the Hebrew Bible, and that this was his perfect word; it required no supplement, only direct implementation in the life of the individual and the community. The Pharisees, on the other hand, thought that revelation was a two-way process, comprising God's word and human response; consequently, the Written Torah had to be complemented by an Oral Torah. This comprised the sum of human responses to God's word, developing, generation by generation, into a science of interpretation of God's intentions and a record of solutions to problems that had arisen in the long passage of time. Thus the key word in Pharisee thought was 'interpretation', or, in the Hebrew expression, 'searching' (*midrash*) of the Scriptures, so that their inner intention could be progressively discovered. This process of 'searching', as the word implies, is a fallible one. It lacks the certainty of inspiration, but has instead the value of human effort and cooperation. Instead of the lonely certainty of the prophet, resulting in an inspired but often obscure text, there was to be a communal effort of enquiry, producing through clear thinking and concerted endeavour an intelligible meaning that would work in practice. Thus the loss of inspiration involved in the closing of the canon was not thought of negatively, but rather as the beginning of a new period in the history of religion, one characterized by human rather than divine values.

Traditions and innovations

Which was the older party, the Sadducees or the Pharisees? It is often said that the Sadducees were the older party, since they

4

based their faith on the established authority of the Bible and rejected all innovations. This, however, is a misunderstanding. It is clear from both Josephus and the New Testament, as well as from the rabbinic writings, that many of the extra-biblical teachings of the Pharisees were not new but rather were traditions of great antiquity. Thus it was the Sadducees who were the innovators, because they rejected these traditions on the theoretical ground that they were not to be found in the Bible. They were, in a sense, reformers, who wished to abolish many popular customs and root them out from the practice of the common people. The Pharisees, on the other hand, defended these popular practices, even though they admitted that there was no explicit mention of them in the Bible. A good example is the ceremony known as 'the Rejoicing of the Water-well', observed during the autumn festival of Tabernacles (for a description of this ceremony see Mishnah, Sukkah 4.9–5.4). A water libation was offered during every day of the festival, together with the usual wine libation, which was prescribed in the Torah. (Every ancient sacrifice, Jewish or non-Jewish, was accompanied by a drink-offering, or 'libation', which was poured out on the altar alongside the animal or vegetable offerings. See Numbers 15.4–10 for the wine libations.) The procession in which a golden flagon filled with water from Siloam was brought to the Temple was an occasion for great rejoicing and display, including the playing of flutes and the performance of torch-dances. The Sadducees opposed this practice, and there was a well-known occasion, recorded both by Josephus and the Mishnah, when the Sadducee High Priest contemptuously poured the water-libation at his feet instead of on the altar, and was pelted by the indignant people with the citrons that formed part of the Tabernacles ritual (see Mishnah, Sukkah 4.9 and Josephus, *Antiquities* XIII. 13.5(372)). This incident is instructive, for it shows that the High Priest, although a Sadducee, *normally* carried out the rituals in accordance with Pharisee doctrine, because the pressure of public opinion was on the side of the Pharisees. The water libation was an ancient practice (probably derived from Canaanite rain-making ritual), older than the final text of the Bible from which it was omitted. Such extra-biblical ancient traditions were regarded by the Pharisees as belonging to the Oral Law, indeed to its most ancient stratum known as 'laws deriving from Moses on Mount Sinai' (in Hebrew: *halakhot le-Mosheh mi-Sinai*).

Yet, despite the antiquity of many of their traditions, it would

5

be wrong to think of the Pharisees as conservative and reactionary in comparison with the Sadducees. The truth is almost the opposite: it was the Pharisees, not the Sadducees, who were in the forefront of development and change in Judaism. This was because, unlike the Sadducees, they were not bound by the literal meaning of the Scriptural text. Just as they could diverge from scripture by preserving customs not mentioned there, so they could introduce new customs and interpretations to cope with new problems and circumstances.

The question of authority

The Pharisees can even be regarded as rebels against the *status quo* represented by the Sadducees. But this *status quo* was of relatively recent date. When the Ptolemaic Greeks (ruling from Egypt) took over Palestine in 320 B.C.E they gave the Jewish High Priest a political authority, as their client prince, which the High Priest had never had in the Jewish constitution as described in the Bible. The new authority of the High Priest as both political and religious leader of the Jewish client-state created a reaction and gave rise to movements, culminating in the Pharisees, that sought to return to the biblical scheme of division of powers. In this scheme the King, the High Priest and the Prophet each had a share of authority, and the chief religious authority belonged to the Prophet, not to either the King or the High Priest.

Indeed, the conflict between the Pharisees and the Sadducees can be expressed as being about *leadership*. The Pharisees stood for the leadership of the laity, whereas the Sadducees stood for the leadership of the priesthood. This is an inevitable outcome of their differing attitudes towards the Scriptures. The Pharisees were interested in the *interpretation* of Scripture, whereas the Sadducees were interested only in its *administration*, which they regarded as requiring little or no interpretation. Consequently, the Pharisees developed a class of scholarly interpreters, known as Sages or Scribes, and later as Rabbis, whose qualifications lay not in their birth, ancestry or performance of impressive rites, but solely in their knowledge of the complexities of the Oral Torah, which was a continually growing body of thoughts and decisions. The Sadducees dismissed this class of Sages as unnecessary. Religious leadership, they thought, should lie with the priests, the hereditary class of descendants of Aaron.

The Pharisees, on the other hand, rejected this claim to hereditary authority. In denying the authority of the priesthood, they did not regard themselves as innovators or rebels, but as reasserting the ancient values of Israelite religion. The Pharisee opposition to the pretensions of the priesthood is expressed, for example, in a saying in the Mishnah, 'A learned bastard takes precedence over an ignorant High Priest'. This does not mean that the Pharisees wished to abolish the priesthood, which they regarded as a God-given institution, as evidenced by the Bible, but that they wished the priests to continue to have the same role as they had in biblical times: performers of animal and vegetable sacrifices in the Temple and of expiatory rites on festivals and the Day of Atonement. Moral and religious teaching had not been the responsibility of the priests; nor had they administered the judicial system. In the Torah, Moses is pictured as a prophet and moral leader, but not as a priest. The priesthood was given to his brother Aaron, a comparatively minor figure. Together with Moses, in the administration of justice, were the Seventy Elders, lay leaders chosen for their wisdom (Numbers 11.16–17). These were the precursors of the Great Sanhedrin, which was regarded by the Pharisees as ideally the supreme religious authority, whereas Moses himself was the model for the Sage or Rabbi. Moses, in addition, had the gift of divine inspiration, which the Pharisees did not claim; they believed that this gift had ceased with the last of the biblical prophets, Malachi, and would return only with the coming of the Messiah. But, although they lacked the gift of prophecy, they did not regard themselves as essentially different in function from Moses and his successors, the Judges and Prophets. Just as the High Priests were the successors of Aaron, so the Sages were the successors of Moses, and were thus entitled to instruct the High Priest in his duties, rather than to submit to his authority.

It is thus very important for the understanding of Jewish religion in the first century not to exaggerate the religious importance of the High Priest. It is natural for a modern reader of the New Testament, for example, to think of him as the Jewish equivalent of the Pope in Roman Catholicism, or the Archbishop of Canterbury in the Church of England. This, however, is a mistake. In Christianity the priests combine the sacerdotal (priestly) and teaching roles, whereas in Judaism they are separate. It is therefore hard to understand a situation in which the sacerdotal head, who took the leading role in the most impressive rituals of Judaism, was nevertheless regarded by the vast majority of Jews (a small minority of Sadducees dissenting) as an ignorant person with nothing to say in matters of faith or doctrine. Indeed, he was regarded as highly suspect in matters of doctrine, being a member of a heretical group, the Sadducees. This did not invalidate his performances in the role of High Priest in the ritual of the Temple, for no great qualities of personality were required for such a role. He was a ceremonial functionary only, and not a source of wisdom or authority. As long as he performed the order of the service correctly, no more was required of him. Only someone descended from Aaron was permitted to perform these ceremonies, and to receive the tithes and other priestly dues. On the other hand, descent from Aaron was not regarded as endowing a person with knowledge. That could be acquired only through hard study, which was available to people of all classes.

The High Priest, nevertheless, was a very important person, not for religious but for political reasons, because the Romans, like their predecessors the Ptolemaic Greeks, gave the High Priest great power as a kind of client prince answerable to them as the occupying force. This was a kind of authority, but not of a spiritual kind. Indeed, the attitude of the Jewish populace towards the High Priest was not one of reverence, for in addition to being an ignorant man, and a Sadducee heretic, he was also the appointee of Roman power—for not only did the Romans give the High Priest power, they actually selected him and appointed him to office. Thus the High Priest who handed Jesus over to the Romans, fearing that his activities would offend the Roman occupying officials (John 11.48), was not acting on behalf of Jewish religion, which he did not represent, but in his capacity as a Roman-appointed police chief.

The Pharisees, on the other hand, being the guardians of popular tradition and the creators of new developments in Judaism, were suspicious of all sources of power, whether in the form of Kings, High Priests or Roman invaders. In this policy of criticism, they were following in the footsteps of the biblical prophets, who were always ready to rebuke the kings and other secular leaders of their time. Elijah the prophet was called by King Ahab 'the disturber of Israel' (1 Kings 18.17), and similarly Josephus describes the Pharisees as 'people who have the greatest capacity for acting against kings' (*Antiquities* XVII. 2.4(41)). Josephus also says, '... the Sadducees are able to persuade none but the rich, and have not the populace obsequious to them, but the Pharisees have the multitude on their side' (*Antiquities* XIII. 10.6). Just as in the case of the High Priesthood, the Pharisees did not want to abolish the Jewish monarchy, which had biblical sanction, but to keep it within its due bounds and to prevent it from claiming any authority of a religious kind not granted to it in Jewish tradition. For this reason, the Pharisees were frequently at loggerheads with the Hasmonean kings, who claimed more than royal authority by combining the throne with the High Priesthood, which the Pharisees regarded as an illegal and unconstitutional amalgamation of functions that should be kept separate. Later, the Pharisees clashed at times with Herod, who usurped the throne of the Hasmoneans. Yet, since they did not oppose the monarchy on principle, the Pharisees could sometimes cooperate with it harmoniously, if the monarch happened to be someone who supported Pharisee doctrines and did not step beyond the constitutional powers granted to the monarchy by the Bible. For example, during the reign of Queen Salome Alexandra (76–67 B.C.E.) regarded later as a golden age, there was harmony between the Pharisees and the monarchy; just as, in biblical times, the reign of Hezekiah had been a rare example of full cooperation between King and prophet.

Later still, when the Romans abolished the Jewish monarchy and turned Judaea into a minor province of the Roman Empire, the Pharisees were prepared, on the whole, to endure this loss of freedom as long as the Roman invaders respected the Jewish religion. But when Jewish sanctities were outraged, as in the time of Pontius Pilate and later of Caligula, the Pharisees adopted a policy of resistance. One extreme wing of the Pharisees, known as the Zealots (see chapter 2), formed an outright resistance movement aiming at the military overthrow of the Romans. At no time did the Pharisees acknowledge the right of the Romans to abolish the ancient Jewish constitution or to reign over the Jews. The Pharisees continued to hope for the restoration of Jewish independence and of Jewish institutions. The hope for the coming of a Messiah was essentially a hope for the restoration of the Jewish state, under its king (the Messiah), its High Priest and its religious establishment (the Sages), headed, if God so willed, by a prophet.

We see that there was a fundamental point of principle at stake in the conflict between the Pharisees and the Sadducees. This was the question of the validity of the Oral Torah—a question that involved many other matters of importance, including the style of leadership required for the implementation of the Jewish religion. But how did the *content* of Pharisaism differ from that of Sadducaism? What differences in practical morality arose from the concept of the Oral Torah? And why do we find such a hostile picture of the Pharisees in the New Testament, where they are accused of hypocrisy, malevolence and meanness? These questions will occupy us in later chapters. Now we must turn to consider the religious scene as a whole among the Jews in this period.

2

The Religious Scene

So far, as an introduction to the religious problems of the period, we have looked at the basic religious difference between the Pharisees and the Sadducees, the two most prominent groupings among the Jews of the first century. Now, however, we must seek a more comprehensive picture of the entire range of Jewish beliefs and groupings from a more descriptive angle. How was the Jewish people, in its entirety, divided among the various religious groups? How were the various groups organized, and to what extent did they exercise authority in the Jewish world? What was distinctive about each one's outlook, and how did they relate themselves to the rival groups and to the Jewish people as a whole?

The Pharisees

The Pharisees, as Josephus says, had 'the multitude on their side', and thus the great majority of the Jews of Palestine must be regarded as followers of Pharisaic Judaism (for the Jews outside Palestine, see section on Diaspora Judaism). But this does not mean that they were all called 'Pharisees'. It seems from both Josephus and the New Testament that this name was confined to the leaders of the movement, who numbered about 6000 (*Antiquities* XVII. 2.4(42)). Josephus himself distinguishes between the Pharisees and the 'people' or 'multitude', and this terminology is found also in the rabbinic literature, in which (although the name 'Pharisee' itself is rarely found), we find a distinction between the 'learned and wise' (*talmid hakham*) and the 'people of the land' ('*am ha'aretz*).

Other names by which the Pharisees were known were 'Sages' and 'Scribes'. The name 'Sages' is that preferred in the rabbinic literature, where every majority opinion is expressed as 'The Sages have said ...'. The name 'Scribes', found frequently in the Gospels, is also found sometimes in the rabbinic literature. Ezra is often called 'Ezra the Scribe', and a fairly common expression is 'the words of the Scribes' (*dibhrei ha-sopherim*), meaning 'rabbinical ordinances' (as opposed to biblical commandments). It is something of a puzzle to scholars that the New Testament frequently uses the paired expression 'Pharisees and Scribes'. This might suggest that the Pharisees were different people from the Scribes; and yet this pairing also suggests that they were closely connected. The best explanation is that the word 'Scribes', as used in the Gospels, refers to the leading Sages, whereas the word 'Pharisees' refers to the rank-and-file of the teachers, including second-ranking Sages and disciples.

The Pharisees were thus a three-tiered movement consisting of Sages, rank-and-file Pharisees, and 'people of the land'. It should be emphasized that the 'people of the land' formed an integral part of this religious structure. A Pharisee prayer, attributed to 'the rabbis of Jabneh' (i.e. to the period 70–100 C.E.) expresses the relationship between the 'learned' and the 'people of the land' as follows:

> I am a creature of God and my neighbour is also His creature; my work is in the city and his is in the field; I rise early to my work, and he rises early to his. As he cannot excel in my work, so I cannot excel in his work. But perhaps you say, I do great things, and he does small things. We have learnt that it matters not whether a person does much or little if only he directs his heart to heaven.
>
> (Babylonian Talmud, Berakhot 17a)

(For more about the Babylonian Talmud, see section on Diaspora Judaism.)

Much that has been written about the relationship between the Sages and the 'people of the land' is misinformed. There was no gap of antagonism between the two groups. The Sages regarded the 'people of the land' as their flock, to whom their sermons were addressed. It was from the 'people of the land' that the Sages themselves came, and any young person who was filled with a sense of vocation could move from the status of 'people of the land' to that of Sage simply by undergoing the necessary course of higher education. The Pharisees never regarded themselves as a sect, but as the religious leaders of the whole people.

The 'people of the land' were not regarded as wicked because they did not seek a state of continual ritual purity; this was never expected or required of them, except at festival time in Jerusalem (see chapter 8). Naturally, relations between the Sages and the 'people of the land' were not always ideal. A few intemperate expressions of irritation uttered by Rabbis of the unsettled period after the Bar Kokhba revolt (132–5 C.E.) have been taken out of context, and the far more numerous expressions of mutual love throughout our period have been overlooked.

The Pharisees were strongly represented in the highest counsels of the nation. In the Sanhedrin, the supreme religious body, they frequently had a majority over the Sadducees. Two examples of this are given in the New Testament, the trial of Peter and his companions (Acts 5) and the trial of Paul (Acts 23). It is only in the deliberations of the Sanhedrin that the Pharisees are seen as a *party*. Outside the Sanhedrin, they were not a party, but the religious leaders of the overwhelming majority of the nation. The Sadducees had powerful representation in the Sanhedrin because of their wealth and aristocratic birth, but in the nation as a whole they did not have a religious following. The other religious parties described below had no representation in the Sanhedrin, and also no national following.

Some interesting encyclical letters, written in Aramaic by Gamaliel I (the same Gamaliel who is mentioned in Acts 5) have been preserved in the Talmud. These letters show the wide range of his influence in the Jewish world as leader of the Pharisees, for he gives instructions about the calendar of the religious year to the Jews of North and South Palestine, and also to the Jews of 'Babylonia, Media and all the other exiled children of Israel' (Babylonian Talmud, Sanhedrin 11b).

Although the Pharisees were religious, not political, leaders, they could not help taking a political role from time to time, like the Hebrew prophets from whom they took their inspiration. In previous times, they had come into conflict with the Hasmonean kings and with Herod I. In the first century too, they continued their active role as critics of established power. The New Testament gives evidence of their opposition to the High Priest (see above), and Josephus also describes how they protested to the Roman authorities about the High Priest's unjust execution of James, the brother of Jesus (*Antiquities* XX. 9.1(197–203)), with the result that the High Priest, Ananus, was deposed from office. (Josephus does not state explicitly that the opponents of the High Priest on this occasion were the Pharisees, but his description of them as 'those most concerned about infringement of the laws' leaves little doubt that the Pharisees were meant.) Here the Pharisees followed their usual policy of defending the Jerusalem Church against the High Priest. Josephus further relates how Simeon ben Gamaliel, son and successor of Gamaliel I, took an important part in the war council of the nation at the time of the Jewish War against Rome (*Life* 38(191–92)).

The chief Pharisee leaders before the Destruction of the Temple (70 C.E.) were Hillel and Shammai (30 B.C.E to 10 C.E.); Gamaliel I (died about 65 C.E.); Simeon ben Gamaliel I (probably executed by the Romans, 70 C.E.); and Johanan ben Zakkai, disciple of Hillel and colleague of his successors. For his activity after the Destruction, see chapter 11.

For the Pharisee sub-groups known as the Hasidim and Zealots, see the sections later in this chapter.

The Sadducees

The Sadducees comprised only a few thousand people, including both leaders and followers, so they can be described correctly as a party or sect. But their political power was out of all proportion to their number, since they were persons of wealth and rank, and had the backing of the supreme political power which, in our period, was that of Rome, and, in previous periods, had been that of the Jewish monarchy of the Hasmonean and Herodian dynasties. The leader of the Sadducees, the High Priest, was appointed to his office by the Romans. As a spiritual leader, he was accepted only by his fellow-Sadducees, and these did not include more than a minority of the priests, for the rank-and-file priests were followers of the Pharisees.

The High Priest acted as President of the Sanhedrin, but here he was often little more than a figurehead, for he and his supporters were frequently voted down by the Pharisees. But it seems that there was a separate political council, or police court, in which the High Priest's power was absolute, since it consisted entirely of Sadducees. This court acted with the backing of Roman power, and cross-examined suspected trouble-makers, such as Jesus.

After the destruction of the Temple in 70 C.E., the Sadducees quickly disappeared from history, as there was no longer any High Priest to lead them, and the Temple had been the centre of their religious life. It may be, however, that the movement called the Karaites, which came into being in the 9th century C.E. as opponents of rabbinic Judaism, derived their back-to-the-Bible doctrine from an undercurrent of Sadducee teaching that survived from Temple times. Some Karaites have survived until the present day.

Unfortunately, we do not have any literature surviving from the Sadducees, and all that we know about them derives from their opponents the Pharisees, and from Josephus and the New Testament. It should be stressed that the Sadducees, although somewhat corrupted by power and wealth, had a sincere religious viewpoint of their own; and even their collaboration with the Romans had good practical reasons. Despite their differences, the Pharisees and the Sadducees reached a working compromise, and did not excommunicate each other. When the Jewish War began in 66 N.E., the Sadducees, despite their previous policy of collaboration with Rome, joined in the war-effort and fought bravely. The Sadducees were loyal Jews, adhered to the basic tenets of the Torah, and hoped for Jewish liberation from the pagan yoke.

The Samaritans

Differing from all other Jews in not recognizing the Temple in Jerusalem, were the Samaritans. Instead, they had their own Temple on Mount Gerizim, near Shechem, and regarded this as the true site of the Temple as revealed to Jacob by God (Genesis 33.18).

The rabbinic writings allege that the Samaritans were descended from the Gentiles described in the Bible (2 Kings 17.24–41), who were transplanted to Samaria by the Assyrians after the exile of the northern Ten Tribes in 721 B.C.E. These Gentiles came from 'Babylon, Cutha, Avva, Hamath and Sepharvaim' (2 Kings 17.24); because of the second place-name mentioned here, the rabbinic writings refer to the Samaritans as 'Cuthites', a name never used by the Samaritans of themselves.

Modern scholarship has shown that this rabbinic theory of the origin of the Samaritans is incorrect, being hostile in motivation. The Gentiles transplanted by the Assyrians to Samaria developed a syncretic religion, worshipping the God of Israel together with their own home-gods, as the Bible says. The Samaritans, on the other hand, were pure monotheists. They were descended, in fact, from the Israelites left behind in northern Israel by the Assyrians, who never exiled the whole of the population, but only a proportion of it. These Israelites allied themselves with the Jews who returned from the Babylonian Exile in 538 B.C.E. but, like their forefathers of the Northern Kingdom, they never quite accepted the religious supremacy of Jerusalem, retaining an attachment to their holy place on Mount Gerizim. After a period of tension, the Samaritans built their own Temple on Mount Gerizim at about 330 B.C.E., but this did not yet lead to a split with the main body of Judaism. This split took place only at about 170 B.C.E., after which the Samaritans were regarded as heretics, but still as Jews.

This historical background perhaps explains the important fact that the Samaritans accepted only the Five Books of Moses as holy writ. The Samaritans did not take part in the religious development of the Jews of the Babylonian Exile in the period between the destruction of the First Temple and the Return, when many of the prophetic and historical books of the Bible were edited and included in the canon. On the other hand, the Samaritans' acceptance of the Pentateuch may indicate that much of it was already canonized before the Destruction.

The Samaritans' rejection of the non-Pentateuchal canon had the effect of making them particularly devoted to Moses, who was their sole prophet, whereas in non-Samaritan Judaism Moses was the first of a long line of prophets.

At the same time, it should be stressed that non-Samaritans too made a great distinction between the authority of Moses and that of the other prophets. In Pharisee tradition, for example, only the Pentateuch was given the title of 'Torah', and the other two sections, the Prophets and the Writings, were of lesser inspiration. In matters of religious law, the Torah was supreme, and nothing in the later books was regarded as superseding or equalling in importance its pronouncements. Thus the gap between the Samaritans and the others was not quite as wide as it appears. Even the Oral Torah was not entirely alien to the Samaritans who, although rejecting the authority of the Pharisee Sages, observed some extra-biblical ordinances that survived from pre-exilic times; for example, they observed the dietary law that forbade the eating of meat and milk products at the same meal (a prohibition only tenuously derived from the Torah's commandment, 'Thou shalt not seethe a kid in its mother's milk').

The Samaritan Temple was destroyed by the Jews under their warlike king John Hyrcanus in 128 B.C.E., and this confirmed the Samaritans in their opposition to Jerusalem. They even altered the text of the Pentateuch, inserting a reference to the holiness of Mount Gerizim in the Ten Commandments. They stood aside from the reforming developments of the Pharisee movement, and their cult, being so rooted in the concept of a Temple, was based entirely on the leadership of the Temple priesthood. This

16

made their outlook rather like that of the Sadducees, whom they also resembled in their denial of the Pharisee doctrine of the resurrection of the dead. But the Sadducees were able to cooperate with the Pharisees to a much larger extent, because of their common attachment to Jerusalem. Also, the Samaritans much limited their religious perspective by their non-acceptance of the prophetic writings, which the Sadducees accepted. Further, the Samaritans prided themselves on the authenticity of their priests, who, they claimed, probaby correctly, were of the true Zadokite stock (i.e. descended from Zadok, the High Priest under David and Solomon). Both Pharisees and Sadducees, on the other hand, were willing to accept High Priests of non-Zadokite stock, such as the Hasmoneans. The Qumran sect (see below) was also concerned about this matter, and resembled the Samaritans in insisting on the Zadokite stock for the High Priesthood.

During the first and second centuries, the Samaritans were accepted as Jews for many legal purposes by the Pharisees (see chapter 10), but the slanderous name 'Cuthites' (alluding to their alleged idolatrous origin) was gaining ground and is found in the works of Josephus, written about 90 C.E. By the third century the Samaritans were regarded as idolaters by the Pharisees, who alleged that idolatrous worship was conducted at Mount Gerizim. It may be that this refers to a form of gnosticism that had developed among the Samaritans during the first century, as attested by the New Testament in its references to Simon Magus (Acts 8.9–11).

The Samaritans have survived as a small sect to the present day in Nablus, on the West Bank, their cult being protected by the state of Israel. They continue to offer animal sacrifices on Mount Gerizim, unlike mainstream Judaism, which discontinued animal sacrifice when the Jerusalem Temple was destroyed in 70 C.E.

The Essenes

We find in certain sources references to a monastic religious group called the Essenes. The meaning of this name is not certainly known, but it may be derived from the Aramaic *'assaya*, meaning 'healers'. Josephus regards the Essenes as an important group, numbering about 4000 in Palestine, and this number is confirmed by Philo (*Probus* 75). There is also a reference to them in the writings of the Roman writer Pliny the

Elder (23–79 C.E.). There is no certain reference to them, however, in the rabbinic writings.

The Essenes differed from other Jewish groups in their separation from ordinary society. They formed communities of their own away from areas of dense population, and bound their members by a solemn oath. They held all goods in common (like the Jerusalem Church (Acts 2.44)), disapproved of the sacrifices of the Temple, avoided marriage (although Josephus says that one branch of them consisted of married people), and opposed slavery. They laid great stress on ritual purity, and took purificatory baths before their communal meals, which were presided over by priests. Philo, who writes of them with great admiration, adds that they abhorred all forms of war, and also of commerce, and supplied their needs entirely by their own labour.

The Qumran sect

Owing to the discovery of the Dead Sea Scrolls at Qumran in 1947, we now know a great deal about a Jewish sect that led a monastic existence in the Judean desert during the first century. The question immediately arises whether this sect was one branch of the Essenes described by Josephus, Philo and Pliny. Pliny indeed located his Essenes in the Dead Sea area. There are many points of similarity between the Qumran sect and the Essenes, but there are also some points of dissimilarity. It is probable that the Qumran sect were indeed Essenes, and that the reports of the three writers contain inaccuracies that have produced discrepancies. All three tended to describe Jewish groups in terms of Greek philosophical movements, and this could be misleading.

Among the writings discovered at Qumran, there were scattered items of information about the history of the sect. It began at about 190 B.C.E. with a group of priests and laymen who 'groped their way' for twenty years until a God-sent 'Teacher of Righteousness' showed them the true way, and was thus the real founder of the sect. The 'Teacher of Righteousness' (not otherwise named) quarrelled with the official Temple priesthood, and led his followers to Damascus where he founded a 'new Covenant', and where he died. Later the sectarians, or some of them, settled in Qumran, where they established their monastic way of life. The settlement was finally destroyed by the Romans in 69 C.E., during the Jewish War against Rome.

The Qumran sect was one of the many Jewish sects of this period whose outlook was 'apocalyptic' (see next section). This term (meaning 'revelatory') expresses the fact that these sects and their writings were inspired by a vision of the Last Days, shortly to commence. The Qumran sect is the best known of the apocalyptic sects because a whole library of writings belonging to it was discovered. This gives us knowledge not only of the beliefs of the sect, but also of its practices and organization, knowledge that we do not have about the apocalyptic sects which gave rise to the writings (Pseudepigrapha) dealt with in the next section.

Nearly all of the Qumran writings testify to the apocalyptic vision of the sect. Among these writings are the following.

1. *The War Scroll*. This describes the order of battle in the final war against the foreign nations, led by the *Kittim* (the Romans, identified as the enemies mentioned in Daniel 11.30–12.3). Jerusalem would be liberated after six years, but the war would last forty years altogether, ending in the triumph of the forces of light, led by two Messiahs, the kingly Messiah and the priestly Messiah.

2. *The Temple Scroll*. This describes the new Temple that would be built in the Messianic age. All the sects, including the Pharisees, expected this, so it was by no means blasphemous of Jesus, as messianic claimant, to declare an intention to destroy and rebuild the Temple (Matthew 26.60), although of course the High Priest would not be pleased at this threat to his regime.

3. *Books of Rules*. The *Manual of Discipline* (or *Community Rule*), gives the aims of the sect and its rules of discipline, by which ritual purity was enforced and strict degrees of initiation were to be traversed by members of the sect, with penalties for any infringements of the regulations. The *Messianic Rule* adds how these arrangements will be supplemented in the coming days of the kingly Messiah and the priestly Messiah. The Priests and the Levites are given leadership in both Rules. The *Damascus Rule* (which was discovered in one version in Cairo in 1910 in a medieval store of documents) gives a summary of the history of the sect, as well as a legal code for its everyday running.

4. *Commentaries on the Bible*. These examine biblical passages to show how they prophesy the advent and role of the Qumran sect itself in the unfolding scenario of the Last Days. This type of apocalyptic biblical commentary is called *pesher*, and is to be distinguished from rabbinical *midrash*, which is

concerned to apply biblical interpretations to the problems of ordinary living, and is relaxed enough to allow for differences of opinion among different interpreters. An example of *pesher* is the Qumran commentary on the first two chapters of Habakkuk, interpreting the Chaldeans as the Romans sent by God to punish the Hasmonean king-priests for their persecution of the Teacher of Righteousness.

5. *Liturgy*. The Qumran texts include hymns of thanksgiving, psalms and blessings used in the liturgy of the sect. Some fragments are mystical hymns ascribed to angels who sing them in their worship of God in heaven.

The Qumran sect was strongly opposed to the Pharisees, as well as to the Sadducees who formed the official Temple administration. In fact, it regarded itself as the last righteous remnant of Israel, which would alone survive the apocalyptic war that lay ahead. They had withdrawn into the desert in repudiation of all other Jewish sources of authority, which they expected to be destroyed.

When the Dead Sea Scrolls were discovered, much excitement was aroused by the prospect that they would throw light on the origins of Christianity. Certainly, they show that messianic expectations were common in this period. The Scrolls also contain many sayings similar to New Testament sayings, but this came as a surprise only to those unfamiliar with rabbinic and pseudepigraphic writings where such sayings are also found, being part of the general thinking of the Judaism of the time.

Yet the Qumran sect has little in common with Jesus' messianic movement. The sect centred on the priesthood and the Temple: even its Messiah is a priestly Messiah, although he was to be accompanied by a kingly figure of the House of David, who would be his executive arm. Although the Qumran sect withdrew from all participation in the sacrificial cult of the Jerusalem Temple, this was not because they had lost interest in the Temple and its rites. On the contrary, it was because the Temple was so important to them that they withdrew from it; they regarded it as polluted by the imperfection of the official priesthood, and they looked forward to the day when it would be restored to purity. The Temple Scroll describes the ideal Temple of the Qumran sect, and the strict regime in which the whole of Jerusalem would become a Temple area in which ritual impurity would be forbidden.

Meanwhile, the Qumran monastery itself was to act as a temporary substitute for the Temple, and ritual purity was rigidly enforced there. This was quite different from the voluntary table-fellowships of the Pharisees, which did not demand ritual purity as a universal rule for all who hoped to be saved (see chapter 8).

Because of the urgency of their apocalyptic expectations, the Qumran writings adopt an authoritative tone which differs widely from that of discussion and opinion found in the Pharisee writings. No differences of opinion are recorded in the Qumran writings; only categorical pronouncements. There was no time for the patient building-up of procedures of discussion and decision-making; the End was too near. Something of this sense of urgency can also be seen in the New Testament, but the Jesus messianic movement is otherwise close to Pharisaism, in its lack of emphasis on the role of the priesthood, its story-telling and its concentration on moral rather than ritual considerations.

The Qumran sect's name for themselves was 'sons of Zadok', which shows the same concern for priestly descent as that shown by the Samaritans, as remarked above. But it is interesting that the Sadducees too probably derive their name from 'Zadok'. It seems that the Sadducees at one time believed that the High Priest must be descended from Zadok, but they compromised on this issue and accepted non-Zadokite High Priests. Since many of the Qumran laws, especially in connection with ritual purity, are curiously similar to those of the Sadducees, it is a possible theory that the Qumran sect was originally a branch of the Sadducees, which broke off in protest against the growing corruption and willingness to compromise of the Sadducee leadership.

Thus the Qumran community differs in some respects from the Essenes described by Josephus, Philo and Pliny, despite some obvious similarities. For example, the abhorrence of war ascribed to the Essenes by Philo does not accord with the Qumran document the War Scroll, which plans for a holy war. The Qumran sect does not disapprove of sacrifices, like Philo's Essenes, but only of the way the sacrifices are conducted by the corrupt priesthood of Jerusalem. As suggested above, the three writers were perhaps presenting an idealized version of the Essenes. In Philo's case, his account was perhaps coloured by his acquaintance with the monastic sect of Therapeutae in Egypt (see page 32).

In one important way, the Dead Sea Scrolls have been held to throw light on the New Testament. The Epistles of Paul and the Gospel of John show a cosmic dualism—a battle on a world scale between Good and Evil, or between Light and Darkness—that had been thought by some to show the influence of Hellenistic dualistic sects. Since the discovery of the Dead Sea Scrolls, however, with their dualistic picture of a battle between good and evil forces in the imminent Last Days, scholars have tended to see a Jewish background for the dualism of New Testament writings; this approach has been supplemented by reference to dualistic tendencies in the pseudepigraphic writings such as 1 Enoch.

It may be doubted, however, whether the dualism of the Dead Sea Scrolls or the Pseudepigrapha is in the same category as that of the New Testament. The Jewish writings do envisage a battle between good and bad angels, but this cosmic struggle is always regarded as a reflection of the struggle between good and bad human beings on earth, and the resolution of the conflict is always an earthly one. That the human conflict is, on the contrary, merely a reflection of a primary cosmic conflict between vast forces of Good and Evil, to be settled on a cosmic, spiritual plane dwarfing human concerns, is a concept alien to all the Jewish writings, which retain the vision of an earthly kingdom of God, peaceful, prosperous and just, as described by the Hebrew prophets.

The Apocalyptists

This leads us into a consideration of the apocalyptic writings of the Pseudepigrapha, and of the kind of first-century Judaism that they represent. The term 'Pseudepigrapha' expresses the fact that these writings were usually ascribed to the authorship of some great figure of ancient Israel such as Enoch or Moses. The term 'apocalyptic' expresses the fact that these writings, whether wholly or in part, contain a revelation of the Last Days, showing how the redemption of the world will proceed. Many of these writings were composed before our period, but they continued to be influential in the first century, as is shown, for example, by the discovery of a copy of the Book of Jubilees, written in the second century B.C.E., among the writings of the Qumran sect. The Book of Jubilees was revered as an inspired work by the sect, who followed it in their observance of a solar calendar (see chapter 7). One of the apocalyptic writings, indeed, was included even in the Pharisee canon. This was the Book of Daniel, a pseudepigraphic work purporting to be written by Daniel in the sixth century B.C.E., but actually written in the second century B.C.E. during the persecution of Antiochus Epiphanes. A New Testament work that belongs to the genre of apocalyptic literature is the Book of Revelation, which represents the viewpoint of Jewish rather than Hellenistic Christianity, and, like the Jewish apocalypses, envisages an earthly messianic kingdom.

It is quite possible that some of the apocalyptic literature may have been composed by members of the Qumran sect; in particular, 1 Enoch 92–105 (sometimes called 'the Epistle of Enoch') shows a strong affinity to the sect's ideas. This and other sections of 1 Enoch were actually found at Qumran, and formed part of the library of the sect. It may have been a production of the sect in its early days in the second century B.C.E.

One apocalyptic work not found at Qumran is particularly interesting because of its possible relationship to the ideas of early Christianity. This is the Parables (or 'Similitudes') of Enoch (1 Enoch 37–71), which was written probably at the beginning of the first century C.E.. Like many of the apocalyptic writings, this describes a heavenly journey, in which Enoch ascends to the throne-room of God, and there receives a revelation about the Last Days. He is also introduced to a figure called the Son of Man, also called 'the Elect One' and 'the Anointed One', who appears to be a conflation of the Son of Man of Daniel 8.15, 9.21, 10.5, the Suffering Servant of Isaiah 53, and the Davidic Messiah. This figure has the role of Judge over the whole world (including the angels) in the Last Days. Yet the final outcome envisaged is an earthly kingdom, ruled over by the Son of Man as an earthly king. The theory that this work was written by a Christian author is now regarded as implausible, but it throws light, despite its many problems, on the milieu in which Christianity arose. It seems that the Son of Man here described is essentially a human figure, given great power by God and able, like Enoch, to ascend to heavenly regions, but never abandoning his human status. (The chapter in which he is identified as Enoch himself is probably a later addition.)

We may thus conclude that there were many apocalyptic sects, each with its special characteristics, although we have detailed knowledge of only one, the Qumran sect. These sects arose in times of great desperation, when the Jews suffered foreign invasion and loss of independence, and when the great hopes of a world converted to monotheism, with the Jews occupying an honoured place as the people of God and his priest-nation, seemed shaken. Apocalypticism was different from biblical prophecy in that it laid down a definite, inevitable programme for future events, rather than seeking to control events by moral exhortation and action. Its lack of genuine prophetic power and confidence is shown by its pseudepigraphic method. Also, it tended to rely on the concept of a saved 'remnant', thus condemning the mass of the world's population, including the majority of the Jewish people, to annihilation in the battles at the end of the world. But it kept alive the hope of a better world, and never abandoned this world as the scene of human destiny.

The Zealots

Although the Pharisees were more level-headed than the apocalyptists, and were prepared to find a way of living in the world as it was (rejecting the apocalyptic writings, with the one exception of Daniel), they were not without apocalyptic hopes of their own. Their attitude towards messianic movements was one of cautious sympathy, as shown by Gamaliel (Acts 5) when he advised the Sanhedrin that, despite the failure of the messianic leaders Judas of Galilee and Theudas, the Jesus movement might turn out to be 'of God'.

This cautious 'wait and see' attitude was typical of the main body of the Pharisees, but from time to time they too erupted into messianic movements. The Zealot movement was the activist, messianic branch of the Pharisees during our period. This is shown by Josephus' statement, 'These men agree in all other things with the Pharisaic notions; but they have an inviolable attachment to liberty, and say that God is to be their only Ruler and Lord' (*Antiquities* XVIII. 1.6.(23)). The founder of the movement was Judas of Galilee, who was himself probably a rabbi (since Josephus calls him *sophistes*, or 'sage') and whose partner, Zadok, was known as 'Zadok the Pharisee'. Judas fought as a guerrilla leader against the Romans with some success. The realistic tone of the Pharisee movement was such that even when a Pharisee embarked on a messianic programme, he did so usually in a realistic way, not relying on a God-given miracle, or on an apocalyptic timetable, but planning a military campaign. On the other hand, it would be wrong to overemphasize this aspect and come to the conclusion that the Zealots were purely political and patriotic in motivation; they were primarily believers. Their name itself proves this, for it was derived from Phinehas the Zealot, the son of Aaron, who was 'zealous for his God' (Numbers 25.13) with sword in hand. It was believed that Phinehas, as a reward for his zeal, had never died, and was identical with Elijah the prophet, who would come back one day to act as forerunner of the Messiah (Malachi 4.5). The Zealots were thus messianists, but they believed that God would help those who showed themselves willing to risk their lives in battle, not those who waited passively for a miracle, or a fore-ordained event.

One of Jesus' disciples was known as 'Simon the Zealot' (Luke 6.15). Simon Peter too may have belonged to the Zealots before joining Jesus' movement, for he had the nickname 'Bar-jonah' (Matthew 16.17); this is derived from the Aramaic *baryona*, meaning 'outlaw', a term often applied to the Zealots.

Judas of Galilee was succeeded in his activities by his sons. Two of these, James and Simon, were executed by the procurator Tiberius Alexander, himself a renegade Jew. A third son, Menahem, took an active part in the Jewish War against Rome, but was killed by his own men when he tried to assume royal honours as Messiah. Evidently, the Zealots were anti-monarchists, who believed so strongly in the kingship of God that they were not willing to accept any earthly monarch. There were many types of messianic belief among the Jews during the first century. The belief in the coming of a royal Davidic Messiah was the commonest, but it was not regarded as heretical to see the messianic age as a republican one, like the age of the biblical Judges.

The Zealots had some successes against the Romans, including their great victory against the army of Cestius Gallus at Beth-Horon (66 C.E.), the event that encouraged the continuance of the war against Rome which ended in national disaster in 70 C.E. The Zealots were not entirely unrealistic in pitting themselves against the might of Rome. They hoped that the Empire would break into warring fragments, as the empire of Alexander had done, and in 69 C.E., the 'year of the four Emperors', this seemed quite likely. In such circumstances, with the previous example of Judas Maccabaeus always before their eyes, the Zealots hoped that an independent Jewish state could be carved out, perhaps with the aid of the Parthian Empire, Rome's chief rival. But the Zealots' hope lay in their faith in God's help. Even after defeat, their faith was so strong that they performed great feats of endurance in martyrdom, refusing, as Josephus describes, to abjure their God even under extreme torture (*Jewish War* VII. 10.1(418)). The heroic defence of Masada, where the surviving Zealots fought to the death, is well known.

But the stubborn courage of the Zealots led only to disaster. The future of Judaism lay not with them, but with the more moderate Pharisees, who made peace with Rome, and built up their religious organisation once more under Johanan ben Zakkai at Jabneh after the War (see chapter 11).

The Hasidim

Another very interesting sub-group of the Pharisees was that of the *Hasidim*. This name means 'saints', and in the long course of Jewish history there have been many movements with this name, apart from the first-century movement with which we are concerned. Whenever this name occurs in Judaism, it always signifies the attempt to 'go beyond the letter of the law', to achieve a spiritual and moral standard above what was normally required. The Torah supplies a code of conduct intended for ordinary people, and it is stressed that this code requires no superhuman efforts:

> The commandment that I lay on you this day is not too difficult for you, it is not too remote. It is not in heaven, that you should say, 'Who will go up to heaven for us to fetch it and tell it to us, so that we can keep it?' Nor is it beyond the sea, that you should say, 'Who will cross the sea for us to fetch it and tell it to us, so that we can keep it?' It is a thing very near to you, upon your lips and in your heart, ready to be kept.
> (Deuteronomy 30.11–14)

The first requirement of Judaism was to achieve a just and kindly society, and all spiritual exercises intended to heighten individual spirituality were considered less immediately important than this communal aim. Yet Judaism never closed the door to the achievement of special spiritual aims by gifted individuals, provided that this was not regarded as a substitute for the ordinary duties required by the Torah. Thus Judaism has produced, in every generation, movements and individuals pursuing special spiritual aims, sometimes moral, sometimes mystical; and yet these special aims are always regarded as peripheral to its central concern, which is the establishment of the kingdom of God on earth (see chapter 9).

The Hasidim of the first century were indeed very much individuals, and it is a little misleading to speak of them as a movement, since they did not organize themselves as such. Yet they were a recognizable 'charismatic' type, and in the aggregate formed a distinct group. There cannot have been more than a few hundred of them at the most. They lived a saintly life, and many quaint stories were told about the unexpectedness and spontaneity of the r actions. Although they were not regarded as having the status of prophets, they were regarded as wonder-workers who could bring about miracle cures and could pray effectively for rain in times of drought.

A famous Hasid was Hanina ben Dosa. It is told that once, when deep in prayer, he was bitten by a scorpion—but it was the scorpion that died! The saying became current, 'Woe to the person who is bitten by a scorpion, and woe to the scorpion that bites Hanina ben Dosa!' Other famous Hasidim were Honi the Circle-maker (so-called because once he drew a circle on the ground, in a time of drought, and challenged God by saying that he would not step out of the circle until the rain came; it duly came), Abba Hilqiah, whose wife surpassed him in powers of rain-making, and Hanan the Hidden One, who, in prayer, like Jesus, referred to God as 'Abba' (the Aramaic word for 'father').

There was some tension between these charismatic Pharisees and their more orthodox colleagues. For example, Honi was reproved for his high-handed manner of prayer, and the Hasidic disregard for ordinary health and safety precautions was sometimes criticized (see also chapter 8). Yet the Hasidim were much admired in the Pharisee movement, even though they were regarded as too special to provide a practical model for ordinary people.

First-century Pharisaism allowed for a variety of religious styles, in addition to the norm. Even within the norm, there was room for disagreement and for differences of attitude, for example that between the more lenient House of Hillel and the more severe House of Shammai. In addition to the Hasidic way of charisma there was a more formal and patterned kind of mysticism, based on the study of Ezekiel's vision of God's chariot and of the first chapter of Genesis. Johanan ben Zakkai was regarded as an adept in this mysticism, but our information about it comes almost entirely from later centuries. Another way of being different was to take a vow of some kind, by which a special mode of religious life could be pursued. The biblical Nazirite vow was quite commonly taken in this period, as an expression of thanksgiving or devotion: it involved abstention from wine and from ritual impurity, usually for a period of thirty days. Another way of being different was to undertake the life of one of the religious fellowships or *habhurot*, of which the best-known is the ritual-purity table-fellowship (see chapter 8).

Diaspora Judaism: Babylonia and Egypt

It is estimated that of the seven million Jews living in the first century, about half lived outside Palestine in what is called the *Diaspora* ('dispersion'). The two greatest centres of Diaspora Jewry were Babylonia, in the Parthian Empire, and Alexandria, the great Egyptian Hellenistic city, which alone contained about a quarter of a million Jews. The Jews of Babylonia, in this period, were dependent on Palestine in religious and cultural matters. They were prosperous and generous, and contributed great gifts to the Jerusalem Temple. Their religion was that of Pharisaic Judaism, and they often sent their promising young men to Palestine to study under the Pharisee sages. Hillel himself was of Babylonian origin. At a later stage, in the third century C.E., Babylonian Jewry developed a religious culture of its own, rivalling and even surpassing the academies of Palestine. It was in this later period that the Babylonian Talmud was developed.

The Babylonian Talmud was compiled in Babylonia at abut 500 C.E., but it contains much material preserved from earlier periods. It takes the form of a commentary on the Mishnah, but it presents a wide-ranging report on the state of the Oral Torah up to the date of its composition, drawing on many sources other than the Mishnah. A parallel compilation, completed about 400 C.E., is the Palestinian Talmud, which was composed in Palestine. It is much briefer than the Babylonian Talmud, but often supplies valuable supplementary information. The Mishnah, which forms the basis of both Talmuds, was compiled by Rabbi Judah the Prince at about 200 C.E.

References to the Babylonian Talmud in scholarly works often take a form such as 'b. Berakhot 45a', where:

'b.' is an abbreviation for 'Babylonian Talmud' (if the abbreviation 'y' or 'j' appears instead, this is a reference to the Palestine Talmud, being an abbreviation for 'Jerushalmi' or 'Yerushalmi', its old name);

'Berakhot' is the name of the tractate, or sub-division. The tractates have the same names in the Talmud as in the Mishnah, since the former is essentially a commentary on the latter;

'45a' means the number of the folio in the standard Vilna edition of the Babylonian Talmud, each folio being divided into side 'a' and side 'b'. This folio numbering is found in the Soncino Talmud translation,[1] alongside its own numbering.

---

[1] I. Epstein (ed.), *The Babylonian Talmud* (Soncino Press, 1952).

In the first century C.E., however, it was the Jews of Alexandria who possessed a religious culture rivalling that of Palestine. Jews who served in Alexander's armies had settled in Alexandria ever since its foundation in 332 B.C.E. It was here that the great Greek translation of the Bible, the Septuagint, was begun under Ptolemy II Philadelphus (288–247 B.C.E.), and continued in the second century B.C.E. In the Letter of Aristeas, written about 130 B.C.E. in Alexandria, an account is given of the composition of the Septuagint by seventy-two translators sent to Egypt from Jerusalem by the High Priest, Eleazar. This account is legendary, and was later embellished by miraculous details, which served to give authority to the Septuagint translation, regarded in Alexandria as divinely inspired. Indeed, the Jews of Alexandria had largely lost their knowledge of the Hebrew language and relied on the Greek Septuagint as the foundation of their faith. On this basis, they developed a distinctive form of Judaism, although they never lost touch with the Judaism of Palestine, which the pious Jews of Egypt constantly visited in the festival pilgrimages.

Alexandrian Judaism was marked by its fusion of Hellenistic culture with Jewish faith. The Alexandrian Jews studied the great Greek philosophers, Plato, Aristotle and the Stoics, and also the poets and tragedians, and they sought to show that Judaism could be reconciled with the best insights of Greek culture. The Letter of Aristeas itself shows this ambition, for it portrays the Egyptian king as deeply impressed by Judaism, and, after long conversations with the Jewish sages, praising their wisdom and their concern for justice. Living in constant contact with Hellenistic culture, the Jews of Alexandria felt compelled to justify their own faith in Judaism in terms intelligible to Hellenistic intellectuals. This justification often took a proselytising turn, so that Alexandria became a centre for the propagation of Judaism as a world religion, containing and transcending the wisdom of the Greeks. Whereas the Letter of Aristeas takes a pacificatory tone, proposing a friendly fusion of Judaism and Hellenism, the Jewish literature of our period is sometimes more aggressive, fiercely criticizing pagan beliefs and practices. This tone was prompted by the worsening of relations between the Jews of Alexandria and the Greek population of the city, who resented the prosperity and cultural pretensions of the Jews. It was in Alexandria that the first serious manifestations of antisemitism appeared, including theories of the Jews as agents of an evil cosmic power.

An interesting form of propaganda for Judaism is that of the Sibylline Oracles. The 'Sibyl' was a famous prophetess of Erythrae, in Ionia, Asia Minor, who composed oracles containing prophecies of the future course of world history. A genre of pseudepigraphic literature was that of oracles in the name of this or other Sibyls. Jews followed the example of pagans in composing such oracles, and naturally made them follow the pattern of Jewish apocalyptic thought, foretelling the future victory of monotheism over the world. Christians also later followed this example, and composed Christian oracles in Greek in the name of the Sibyl. Some of the Sibylline oracles composed by Jews appeared in the first century, and use great events, such as the fall of Nero, as signals of the approaching Last Days.

Another production of Alexandrian Jewry was the Wisdom of Solomon, composed probably early in the first century C.E. This pseudepigraphic work combines Greek and Jewish thought. The personification of Wisdom, derived from Proverbs 8, is illuminated by the Greek philosophy of the Logos. It has been thought to have influenced certain aspects of the New Testament, especially in its treatment of the Suffering Servant theme.

Alexandrian Judaism, however, gave rise to purely literary works, as well as to works aspiring to inspired status. A large fragment has survived of a fascinating work, the *Exagoge* of Ezekiel the Tragedian. This is a tragedy, in the style of Euripides, based on the story of the Exodus from Egypt—a natural subject for an Egyptian Jew. But the greatest example of Alexandrian–Jewish literary effort is undoubtedly the work of Philo, the philosopher and biblical exegete. His voluminous works apply an allegorizing method to the exegesis of the Bible, showing how the concepts of Greek philosophy, especially that of Plato, can be discovered in symbolic form in the biblical stories. For example, the conflict between Sarah and Hagar (Genesis 21.9–21) is interpreted by Philo as an allegory of the rival, but complementary, claims of virtue (Sarah) and education (Hagar).

Philo was the first philosopher of Judaism, the precursor of Saadia and Maimonides. These medieval Jewish philosophers, however, did not build their work on Philo, because the latter's works were not preserved by Jews, but by Christians. Philo's allegorical method of interpreting the Bible and his method of theology had great influence on the development of Christian exegesis and theology—so much so that a legend arose in the

Christian Church that Philo, before his death in about 40 C.E., was converted to Christianity. In fact, he was a pious adherent of Judaism all his life.

Philo was careful to warn his readers not to infer from his allegorical method of explaining Jewish laws that these were to be regarded as merely symbolic, and therefore not legally binding in practical observance. He regarded the laws as primarily divine injunctions to be obeyed, but also as having profound meanings, the study of which could raise a person to prophetic insight into the nature of God. Christian exegesis of the Old Testament, however, seized on Philo as providing a way of allegorizing the laws out of practical existence, in accordance with Christian doctrine of the abolition of the Jewish Covenant. Indeed, as it appears from Philo's protests, a few Alexandrian Jews too wished to use the allegorical method to abolish the need for practical observance, so that Jewish assimilation to the Hellenistic environment could be promoted.

Why did Philo's work have so little influence on Judaism itself? Why did Judaism have to wait for another 900 years before the challenge of Greek philosophy was taken up again in the brilliant work of Saadia? The answer lies in the tragic catastrophe that overcame Alexandrian Jewry in 115 C.E., under the Emperor Trajan, when the hostility between Greeks and Jews boiled up into a civil war covering not only Egypt, but also Cyrenaica, Libya and Cyprus. Alexandrian Jewry, the centre of Hellenistic Judaism, was wiped out, never to recover. Other catastrophes followed in other Hellenistic Jewish centres. Rabbinic Judaism was left as the sole remaining standard-bearer for Judaism, and it was not part of its programme to effect a synthesis of Judaism and Greek philosophy. This was certainly not all loss, for there was something alien to Judaism in the Hellenistic conception of God as an abstract Being, devoid of all categories and emotions, communicating with the world through intermediate agencies, the Logos and emanations. In rabbinic Judaism, God is a Loving Father, feeling emotions of love, anger and sorrow; and the philosophical problems of reconciling such a God with the Absolute did not worry the rabbis, at least in their main intellectual labours.

Philo's work is important not only because of its philosophical and exegetical content, but also because of the light it often throws on the history of the period. Philo himself, being a member of a distinguished Alexandrian family, was drawn unwillingly from his studies into the whirlpool of events, when he took a prominent part in the delegation sent by Alexandrian Jewry to the Emperor Caligula in 40 C.E. to plead for the restoration of Jewish rights withheld by the Governor Flaccus under the influence of the Greeks. Philo's long account of the work of this delegation, which had to cope with Caligula's mad pretensions to divine status, is a valuable historical document.

Among his many valuable testimonies concerning Egyptian Judaism is his account of a Jewish sect called the Therapeutae (so-called because of their healing powers). This was a group that led a monastic life, holding all their goods in common, practising asceticism and devoting themselves to prayer and contemplation. The relation of this sect to the Essenes or Qumran sect of Palestine is problematic. It is agreed by scholars, however, that the Therapeutae formed the Jewish origin of the Christian monastic movement, which, as is well known, began in Egypt.

Alexandrian Judaism, in general, forms a distinguished chapter in Jewish history, although in the first century it was approaching its tragic end. The Jews of Alexandria were loyal to the Torah, and were influenced strongly by the Pharisaic Judaism of Palestine, as is shown by their contributions to the Jerusalem Temple, their frequent pilgrimages, their splendid synagogues and their devotion to Pharisaic practices such as the lighting of the Sabbath lights. Their literature in Greek shows a great pride in their Jewish heritage, and a desire to promote Judaism or monotheism as a world religion; they were also very conscious of the superior morality of Judaism as compared with paganism, and spoke out against, for example, the barbarous pagan practice of infanticide.

Despite their loyalty to Palestinian Judaism, the Alexandrian Jews showed an independence and originality that set them apart from the rabbinic Judaism on which all later Judaism was based. One curious expression of this independence was their maintenance of a Temple in Leontopolis (in the region of Heliopolis, in the Delta region of northern Egypt), in violation of Deuteronomic law. This Temple had first been founded in 152 B.C.E. by the priest Onias, a refugee from Palestine, who first conceived his project when the Jerusalem Temple was in the hands of idolatrous renegades, but went ahead with it even after the rescue of the Jerusalem Temple from the pollution of idolatry by the Hasmoneans. The Alexandrians (or some of them) justified their Egyptian Temple from Scripture, which prophesied that there would be an altar in Egypt to the Lord of Hosts (Isaiah

19.18–19), and they never regarded their Temple as equal in status to the Jerusalem Temple; many Egyptian Jews, indeed, disapproved of the Leontopolis Temple altogether. The Pharisees, of course, disapproved of it, but not to the extent of regarding Alexandrian Judaism as schismatic, as in the case of the Samaritans. In Pharisee law, priests who had served at Leontopolis were disqualified from subsequently serving in Jerusalem, yet to a limited extent the sacrifices offered at Leontopolis were regarded as valid (Mishnah, Menahot 13.10). The Leontopolis Temple was finally destroyed by the Roman Emperor Vespasian in 73 C.E., in the wake of the destruction of the Jerusalem Temple.

Other Diaspora communities

In addition to Babylonia and Egypt, Jews lived in many other countries outside Palestine, carried there very often as prisoners of war, but also by voluntary emigration. According to a Sibylline Oracle, 'every land and every sea' was filled with Jews, and the historian Strabo wrote, 'Scarcely any place in the world can be found which has not received members of this race' (quoted by Josephus, *Antiquities* XIV. 7.2(115)). The New Testament mentions Jews as coming from Cappadocia, Pontus, Asia, Phrygia, Pamphylia (all in Asia Minor) and from Rome, Crete and Arabia (Acts 2.9–11). The great numbers of Jews in the Diaspora probably cannot be explained by emigration alone; there was extensive conversion of Gentiles to Judaism during this period.

Large numbers of Jews lived in Antioch, the capital of Syria, and in Rome itself. We have little direct knowledge, however, of the kind of Judaism practised in such centres. Only Alexandria produced a Jewish literature that has survived. Excavations of many Jewish synagogues, however, have shown that they were organized on very similar lines to those of Egypt, Babylonia and Palestine, and we know that the practice of pilgrimage kept them in touch with the Palestinian centre. It seems reasonable to conclude that the Judaism practised was of the Palestinian type, i.e. Pharisaic on the whole (although there is evidence of a Samaritan Diaspora too), but modified by Hellenistic culture, as in Alexandria. Prayer was probably mostly in Greek.

Everywhere the Jews practised their own religious law, observed the Sabbath and the festivals, performed the rite of circumcision, observed the dietary laws, and usually administered their own courts 'according to the ancestral laws', as Josephus says about the Jews of Rome (*Antiquities* XIV. 10.17(235)). The Jews everywhere retained the messianic hope for the liberation of their homeland, Palestine, and the inauguration of a world-wide era of peace under the spiritual direction of Israel, the priest-nation of God.

The theory once held by some scholars that Hellenistic Judaism was far removed from Palestinian Judaism, that it rebelled against observance of the Torah, and that it worshipped with religious symbols derived from pagan cults, is no longer regarded as supported by the archaeological facts.

Were there any Jewish communities, living in isolated places, that preserved forms of Judaism surviving from the period preceding the time of Ezra? We do not know for certain that such communities existed anywhere during the first century. Some have regarded the Ethiopian Jews (*Falashas*) as surviving from such an ancient community, but this is very doubtful.

We do know of one isolated Jewish Diaspora community, with a pre-Ezra kind of Judaism, that existed in the fifth century B.C.E. in Elephantine, in southern Egypt. These Israelites, who were placed in Elephantine by the Persian Empire as a military colony at about 550 B.C.E., practised a synthetic form of religion (of the kind denounced by the Hebrew prophets) combining the worship of the Israelite God with that of a female deity. It is just possible that some isolated communities practising early forms of Israelite religion survived into the first century, but knowledge of this must await further archaeological finds.

Christianity

One Jewish sect that appeared in the first century was the group that centred on the leadership and personality of Jesus. There was nothing in this sect, in its early years, that constituted a radical departure from the Judaism of the period. Jesus himself, in his preaching, conforms closely to the pattern of a Pharisaic teacher (see chapter 3). His use of parables is typical of Pharisee preaching. His emphasis on repentance, forgiveness of sinners and on the coming kingdom of God is very similar to that of Pharisaism, although his sense of urgency and belief that the kingdom was imminent is more reminiscent of the apocalyptic sects, including the Qumran sect. Unlike the Zealots, the messianic wing of the Pharisees, he did not adopt a militaristic posture, organizing guerrilla warfare against the Romans. Jesus appears to have believed that his nationwide campaign of repentance, directed towards 'the lost sheep of the house of Israel', would result in the intervention of God, who would miraculously institute the promised kingdom. In this, Jesus approximates to the messianic type of Theudas, a non-militaristic, charismatic messianic claimant who was crushed by the Romans when his expected miracle did not materialize. (For Theudas, see Josephus, *Antiquities* XX. 5.1.(97–8), and Acts 5.36.)

Accounts of Jesus' conflicts with the Pharisees on questions of Sabbath healing or corn-plucking turn out to be inaccurate when Pharisee law in the rabbinic writings is examined (see chapter 3). Jesus' declaration, 'The Sabbath was made for man, not man for the Sabbath', was a Pharisee watchword. Jesus was not in conflict with the Pharisees on the question of ritual purity (see chapter 8). In fact, he advocated no reform of Jewish law except the reforms already introduced by the Pharisees. Jesus was an observant and loyal Jew. His religion was Judaism, and his faith was based on the Hebrew Bible. It did not occur to him to think of himself as a divine figure. Such a belief would have been, for him, a direct contravention of the first of the Ten Commandments. The fact that Jesus did not advocate any new departure in Jewish religion is proved by the practice of his followers who formed the 'Jerusalem Church' under the leadership of James, Peter and John. These were all pious adherents of Judaism, who observed circumcision, the Sabbath (on Saturday), the dietary laws, the festivals and fasts, the sacrificial cult of the Temple, and the other observances of Pharisaic Judaism. Evidently, nothing that Jesus said to them made them think that these observances were to be discontinued.

Why, then, did a distinctive Christian sect develop? The answer to this lies not in any special or unusual doctrines that Jesus was preaching, but in his, or his followers', claims that he was the Messiah, 'the anointed one'. The Messiah would fulfil the promises of the Hebrew Prophets and liberate the Jews from foreign rule, just as Moses had liberated their ancestors from Egypt, and would thus initiate a new era of peace and justice for the whole world, when the ruling power would be the knowledge of the Lord, not the military might of empires. Those who were attracted by Jesus' charismatic personality, his preaching of repentance and his prodigies of faith-healing, formed the movement of the 'Nazarenes', a movement that was not identical with other messianic movements of the period (for each had its special features), but was equally a product of first-century Judaism.

35

A unique feature of Jesus' messianic movement, however, was that it did not disband after his death. Other messianic movements collapsed with the death of the would-be Messiah; the followers of Theudas, for example, dispersed once Theudas was cut down by the Romans. Many of Jesus' followers did melt away when he was crucified as a trouble-maker by the Romans, with the connivance of the Romans' appointee and police chief, the High Priest. But a core of his followers remained. They were enabled to do so by their belief in Jesus' resurrection. The Nazarenes of the Jerusalem Church believed that Jesus had been brought back to life by a miracle from God. They did not believe that Jesus' resurrection proved him to be a divine being, a concept that would have been repugnant to them as Jews, and their belief in his resurrection did not constitute any heresy on the part of the Nazarenes; on the contrary, as the New Testament itself testifies, their belief was treated with sympathy by Gamaliel, the leader of the Pharisees, who said that it could turn out to be 'of God'. There were many varieties of messianic belief among the Jews, and these beliefs were tolerated even though held by a small minority.

There is a mistaken theory that it would have been heretical to believe in a messiah who had been crucified. This view is based mainly on Paul's conception (Galatians 3.13) that Jesus incurred a curse by being crucified. However, Paul's interpretation of Deuteronomy 21.23 in this sense was not in accordance with any Jewish tradition, but was his own individual idea. Thousands of Jews were crucified by the Romans in the first century, and were regarded by the Jewish people as martyrs, not as being under a curse.[1]

So far, then, the Nazarenes formed part of the scene of first-century Judaism. They formed a distinctive group, with an organization of its own that met regularly for meals and religious services, but thereby did not cut itself off from the totality of Jewish life—for there were many synagogues composed of members with some common interest (see page 61). The Nazarenes took part in the Temple worship, and thus they recognized the Temple priesthood, and had no separate priesthood of their own. They had no notion of belonging to any religion other than Judaism. They entered other synagogues freely, and were regarded by all other Jews as Jews.

[1] See my *Early Rabbinic Writings* (Cambridge University Press, 1988), pp. 195–197.

Modern research has shown that the picture given in Acts and other early Christian literature of Jewish persecution of Christianity is seriously misleading. Acts sometimes contradicts its own picture: for example, in its portrayal of Gamaliel, and in its remark about Ananias of Damascus, a Christian, that he was 'a devout observer of the Law and well spoken of by all the Jews of that place' (Acts 22:12). For extended treatment of this theme, see James Parkes, *The Conflict of the Church and the Synagogue*,[1] Douglas A. R. Hare, *The Theme of Jewish Persecution of Christians in the Gospel according to St. Matthew*,[2] and my own *The Mythmaker*,[3] which argues that those acts of persecution that did take place (e.g. the execution of James, Jesus' brother) were political in character, and were confined to the collaborationist circle of the Sadducees and Herodians.

Christianity developed as a separate religion only when it adopted the doctrine that Jesus was a divine being, and that salvation depended on identification with his sacrificial death, rather than in adherence to the Jewish or Noachian covenants. When this development took place is a controversial question on which many opinions are possible. There can be no doubt, however, that it was through this important change of doctrine that Christianity ceased to be part of the scene of first-century Judaism. Not all Christians, however, accepted this change of doctrine. The history of the Jewish-Christians, called Ebionites or Nazarenes, would take us beyond the first century, but they claimed, probably with good reason, to be the successors of the first Jewish-Christians, the Jerusalem Church.

[1] Soncino Press, 1934.
[2] Cambridge University Press, 1967.
[3] Weidenfeld and Nicholson, 1986.

3

Pharisaic Judaism

The foregoing survey of the varieties of Judaism in the first century shows clearly that by far the most significant and religiously influential kind of Judaism was Pharisaism, which exercised authority over the majority of the Jewish people, both in Palestine and the Diaspora. All the other forms of Judaism were relatively small sects, though one of these, Sadducaism, because of its economic wealth and its relations with the ruling power of Rome, had an importance out of keeping with its numbers. Hellenistic Judaism, though possessing some traits of its own, remained faithful to the authority of the Pharisee leaders of Palestine.

Some scholars recently (see especially the writings of Jacob Neusner) have argued on the contrary that the Pharisees were a small, insignificant group which exercised no authority over the Jewish masses. This view contradicts the evidence of Josephus, the New Testament and the rabbinic writings.

A study of first-century Judaism must therefore be concerned primarily with the doctrines and practices of the Pharisees, to whom we now return.

The New Testament view

We have already seen that certain facts about the Pharisees, found in Josephus and the rabbinic writings, contradict the picture of the Pharisees found in the New Testament. Readers of the Gospels do not gain any strong impression of important differences between the Pharisees and Sadducees. The only point to which their attention is drawn is that the Pharisees believed in the resurrection of the dead, whereas the Sadducees did not (Matthew 22.23; Acts 23.8). The Pharisees and the Sadducees alike are drawn as authoritarian figures, united in their opposition to Jesus. No hint is given that the Pharisees are the party of the people, with a record of fearless opposition to established power. Nor is there any hint that, whereas the leaders of the Sadducees came from the rich and from the hereditary priestly

38

aristocracy, the leaders of the Pharisees were drawn from all strata of society, including the poorest of artisans and agricultural labourers. The nearest the New Testament comes to revealing this is when it describes Gamaliel, the Pharisee leader, as 'held in high regard by all the people' (Acts 5.34). (Indeed, the picture of the Pharisees given in Acts is in several respects at odds with that given in the Gospels.)

We are forced to the conclusion that the picture of the Pharisees given in the Gospels is coloured by hostile motives, and cannot be regarded as historically reliable. At the time when the Gospels were edited, about 40 to 70 years after the death of Jesus, there was conflict between the leaders of the Christian Church and the Pharisees, who in this period were even more the leaders of Jewish religious life than in the time of Jesus. This conflict was not because the early Church was being persecuted by the Pharisees. The baselessness of this traditional charge has been demonstrated by James Parkes in *The Conflict of the Church and the Synagogue*.[1] The real point was that the Hellenistic Christian Church, now consisting mainly of non-Jewish converts, wished to dissociate itself from Judaism, which had become highly unpopular in the Roman Empire because of the Jewish War against Rome. The fact that Jesus was crucified as a troublemaker and presumably a rebel against Roman power was extremely awkward for the Church, which found it imperative to argue that Jesus' enemies had been the Jewish religious leaders, not the Roman authorities.

This conflict was written into the Gospels in the form of conflict between the Pharisees and Jesus himself. When we come to examine these alleged conflicts (on the question of Sabbath healing, for example), we find that they do not make sense in the light of what we know about Pharisee teaching from other sources (see below). We cannot safely conclude from the Gospel evidence that there was any serious conflict between Jesus and the Pharisees at all.

Historical origins

Let us then examine the record of the Pharisees as it can be gleaned from sources other than the Gospels. The name 'Pharisee' (Greek, *pharisaios*) comes from the Hebrew word *parush*, which means literally 'one set apart'. Why did the

[1] Soncino Press, 1934.

Pharisees have this name? The answer is rather complicated. It was *not* because they set themselves apart from the common people, for they were the party of the common people, as shown in the previous chapter, and had very wide popular support. One of the best-known sayings of the great Pharisee sage Hillel was, 'Do not separate yourself from the community'. It is wrong also to say that the word *parush* means 'one who belongs to a ritual-purity table-fellowship' (see chapter 8), although the word *sometimes* has this meaning. The fact is that the word *parush* had many meanings, some complimentary and some uncomplimentary. One of its uncomplimentary meanings was 'sectarian' or 'heretic', and the most probable explanation of the term *parush* in its meaning of 'Pharisee' is that this was originally an uncomplimentary term applied to the party by their opponents, the Sadducees, but later accepted as a name of honour—much as happened in Christian history in relation to the term 'Puritans'. Originally labelled 'heretics' by their opponents because of their opposition to the priesthood, the Pharisees outlived the stigma and became the majority party. After the destruction of the Temple by the Romans (70 C.E.) the Pharisees became so much the dominant party that they ceased to use this name. The Sadducees had faded away, having no *raison d'être* without a Temple; so the Pharisees, now supported by the Jews as a whole, did not require a name to distinguish them from the Sadducees. The leaders of the Pharisees were known as 'sages' (Hebrew, *hakhamim*), and, at a later period, as 'rabbis', from a Hebrew word meaning 'master' or 'teacher'.

The historical origin of the Pharisees can be traced to the period just before the Hasmonean revolt against the Seleucid Greeks, which took place in 168 B.C.E. and reached a victorious outcome in 160 B.C.E. At this time, a corrupt High Priesthood was collaborating with the Hellenizing efforts of the Greek ruler, Antiochus Epiphanes, who was trying to abolish essential beliefs and practices of Judaism. Aiding the Hasmonean family in their revolt was a religious group known as the Hasidim ('pious ones'), and it was this group that almost certainly developed into the Pharisee party. The origin of the Sadducee party can also be traced to this very same period in Jewish history. This was because the issue between the two parties—the status of the priesthood and the Oral Torah—came to a head during this period. It was not a new issue (see chapter 2); but it came to such a point of crisis, because of the corruption of the High Priesthood at this time, that the tension that had always existed between two attitudes in Jewish religion crystallized into the formation of two parties, each with its own name and slogans. The Sadducees, as was appropriate for a priestly party, took their name from that of a prominent biblical High Priest, Zadok, who held that office under King David (2 Samuel 8.17).

Interpretation of the biblical laws

Josephus tells us that 'the Pharisees tend to be lenient in punishments' (*Antiquities,* XIII. 10.6(294)). This is indeed a very important fact about the Pharisees, which is amply borne out by the Pharisaic literature. Because of their concept of the Oral Torah, supplementing the Written Torah, the Pharisees were not bound by the letter of the biblical laws and were able to liberalize and humanize them when necessary. This liberality of interpretation was not open to the Sadducees, whose interpretation of the biblical laws was thus much harsher and more severe. The day, during the reign of the pro-Pharisee Queen Salome Alexandra, when the harsh decrees of the Sadducees were rescinded, was celebrated thereafter by the Pharisees and the people as a public holiday.

A good example of Pharisee humanity in interpreting biblical laws is their interpretation of the biblical principle 'an eye for an eye' (Exodus 21.24). This apparently means that if I knock out my neighbour's eye, my own eye must be knocked out in punishment. The Pharisees, however, did not accept this literal meaning. One of their many objections to such literalism was the question, 'What happens if a one-eyed man knocks out his neighbour's eye?' The punishment, in such a case, would be quite incommensurate with the crime. The Pharisees held that Scripture did not enjoin any such crude retaliation, but was referring to *compensation.* 'An eye for an eye' means, 'Pay compensation to your victim matching the gravity of the injury you have inflicted on him.' It should be noted that Scripture itself enjoins the payment of monetary compensation for an injury inflicted (Exodus 21.19), an injunction impossible to reconcile with a literal interpretation of 'an eye for an eye'.

It may be as well to raise here a point of general importance in relation to Pharisee lenience and humanity. Some scholars, wishing to support and confirm the picture of Pharisee male-volence and violence found in the Gospels, have thrown doubt on the validity of evidence taken from the rabbinic literature. This literature, it is argued, is too late to provide good evidence for the time of Jesus. Thus the arguments against a literal interpretation of 'an eye for an eye' are found in the Babylonian Talmud, which was completed at about 500 C.E., while even the earlier rabbinic literature, the Mishnah and the Tannaitic Midrashim, cannot be dated earlier than 200 C.E. This argument, however, ignores the fact that rabbinic literature is always the end product of a very long process of shaping, and contains material that is of much earlier date than that of the final editing or 'redaction'. This means that the material must indeed be handled with due caution, so that the earlier strata are not confused with the later; but as long as such caution is exercised, the rabbinic literature contains a wealth of priceless material bearing on the first-century period. Also, as it happens, there is one rabbinic work, *Megillat Ta'anit*, which is earlier than all the others, and which provides evidence of Pharisee leniency in contrast with Sadducee severity.

Some scholars have even cast doubt on the *bona fides* of Josephus' testimony to the leniency of the Pharisees, arguing that Josephus was in league with the Pharisees and wished to recommend them to the Romans, and so gives an over-favourable picture of them. This contention too ignores important facts; Josephus, for example, is by no means always favourable to the Pharisees, and he cites disapprovingly their tendency to sedition, a trait that would not endear them to the Romans. In view of Josephus' ambivalent attitude to the Pharisees, sometimes admiring them, but often disparaging them, his testimony to their leniency must be regarded as weighty.

Jesus and the Sabbath laws

Sabbath healing

One charge constantly made against the Pharisees in the Gospels is that they persecuted Jesus because of his Sabbath healing. What truth is there in this charge? All the evidence in the Pharisee writings points to the conclusion that the Pharisees did *not* forbid healing on the Sabbath. In the Mishnah, a compendium of Pharisee law, a list is given of activities that were defined as 'work', and were therefore forbidden on the Sabbath, in accordance with the biblical command (included in the Ten Commandments) 'Six days shalt thou labour and do all thy work: but the seventh day is the sabbath of the Lord thy God: in it thou shalt not do any work' (Exodus 20.9–10). The rabbinic list contains thirty-nine items, comprising the work of agriculture, such as sowing and reaping, and of manufacture, such as weaving or building; but healing does not figure as an item on this list. The rabbis regarded this list of forbidden kinds of work as a very ancient tradition—so ancient that it was regarded as belonging to that part of the Oral Torah that was given to Moses on Mount Sinai together with the Written Torah. This list, or something very like it, was certainly in existence in the time of Jesus. The rabbis also explained that the kinds of work included in the list were also the kinds of work required to build the Tabernacle in the wilderness: this explanation rules out healing as a possible item on any such list.

So far from forbidding healing on the Sabbath out of fear that healing might infringe the prohibition against 'work', the rabbis actually *encouraged* it to such an extent that they said that any or all of the thirty-nine modes of 'work' should be practised on the Sabbath if this conduced to the healing of any dangerous complaint. For example, although lighting a fire was forbidden on the Sabbath (this prohibition, indeed, is found explicitly in the Torah, Exodus 35.3), if an invalid urgently required heat, a fire should be lit even on the Sabbath. If, however, an invalid was not dangerously ill, healing should be practised such as did not involve the infringement of any of the thirty-nine modes of 'work'. In other words, danger to human life overrode all the prohibitions of the Sabbath, and healing itself, even of complaints that presented no danger to life, was not forbidden. At a later stage, probably later than the lifetime of Jesus, the use of medicines for trivial complaints was forbidden, not because of any prohibition against healing as such, but because it was feared that such use might lead to the actual grinding of medicinal ingredients on the Sabbath, which was forbidden. Also, one minority opinion, found in the Mishnah, is that setting a dislocated bone should be forbidden on the Sabbath, as it is more like 'building' than healing, but this was overruled. This is the full extent of restraint on Sabbath healing.

In the case of Jesus' Sabbath healing, it is impossible to find anything in Pharisaic law that would render it forbidden. Jesus' method of treatment was what would nowadays be called 'faith-healing', and did not involve any mode of 'work' such as lighting fires or grinding medicines. Consequently, it was permitted even where there was no danger to life. In the case of some of the more serious complaints that he is reported to have cured, he would have been permitted by Pharisee law to undertake such cures even if an actual breach of the thirty-nine Sabbath prohibitions was involved, for dangerous illness overrode all these prohibitions.

It is even more remarkable that the arguments that Jesus is reported to have used to justify his Sabbath healing are the very arguments that were used by the Pharisee rabbis. For example, one argument ascribed to Jesus was, 'If a child is circumcised on the Sabbath to avoid breaking the law of Moses, why are you indignant with me for giving health on the Sabbath to the whole of a man's body?' (John 7.23). In the Mekilta, an early rabbinic work, we read, 'Rabbi Eleazar ben Azariah said: If in performing the ceremony of circumcision, which affects only one member of the body, one is to disregard the Sabbath laws, how much more should one do so for the whole body when it is in danger!' (Mekilta, Shabbata 1). Rabbi Eleazar ben Azariah flourished about 60 years later than Jesus, but it is evident that the argument he uses was a traditional one in the Pharisee movement; neither Jesus nor he invented it. This kind of argument is very typical of the Pharisees, and Jesus, in using it, is adopting a very typical Pharisee style. Note how he even appeals to Pharisee law, when he points out that the duty of circumcision on the eighth day overrides the Sabbath law, if the eighth day happens to occur on a Sabbath. This is not a decision that can be found in the Bible, which says nothing about a possible conflict between the laws of circumcision and those of the Sabbath; it is in the rabbinic writings that we find the problem considered, and solved in the manner stated by Jesus. So here we find Jesus arguing like a typical Pharisee, yet, allegedly, his opponents on the question of Sabbath healing were the Pharisees!

Perhaps the most celebrated saying of Jesus on the question of Sabbath healing is, 'The Sabbath was made for man, not man for the Sabbath' (Mark 2.27). This has often been extolled as a highly original saying, showing a new attitude towards the observance of the Sabbath, the alleged rigidity of the Pharisees being contrasted with Jesus' flexibility. It will come as a surprise to many readers to be told that this saying too was traditional in the Pharisee movement, and was not invented by Jesus. The saying appears in the same passage of the Mekilta, in the very slightly different form, 'The Sabbath was handed over to man, not man to the Sabbath'. The saying, in both its forms, implies that the Sabbath is a gift to man, which should bring happiness and not pain, and therefore it is against the spirit of the Sabbath to allow its prohibitions to result in danger and death. The saying, however, also implies a positive attitude towards the

Sabbath as a gracious benefit bestowed by God. When Jesus quoted the saying, he was endorsing the Pharisees' flexibility towards the Sabbath, and also their love for it. He was not abolishing the Sabbath, or its laws, but saying that they should be interpreted with humanity, just as the Pharisees argued. Sayings like these raise the question of Jesus' relation to the Pharisee movement, and suggest the probability that he was himself a member of that movement, despite the alleged hostility of the Pharisees towards him.

How can we account, then, for the strange fact that the Gospels record so many instances of Pharisee disapproval of Jesus' Sabbath healing, when research shows that the Pharisees would have actually approved of it, and also that Jesus' arguments and sayings in favour of Sabbath healing are identical with those found in Pharisee sources? It can hardly be the case that these stories have been entirely invented; Jesus must have spent some of his time arguing the case for Sabbath healing against *some* person or persons. It is possible that Jesus' real opponents in this matter were not the Pharisees but the Sadducees, who are known to have applied the Sabbath laws more literally and harshly than the Pharisees, in accordance with their general belief in literal interpretation of the Bible. At a late stage of the editing of the Gospels, the name 'Pharisees' could have been substituted for 'Sadducees' in the Sabbath-healing stories, so that the name of the Pharisees, the chief Jewish opponents of the Christian Church at that later period, would be blackened. At the period in question (*ca.* 70–110 C.E.) the Christian Church was much concerned to assert its loyalty to Rome and to dissociate itself from Jewish rebellion, which had erupted in the Jewish War (66–70 C.E.). Jesus, too, was commonly thought to have been a rebel against Rome, because of his death by crucifixion, the Roman punishment for rebels. Consequently, it had to be asserted that Jesus' enemies were not the Romans, but the Jewish religious authorities, and that he had rebelled not against Rome but against Judaism. For this reason, the Pharisees were portrayed as having wished to kill him for *religious* reasons, although, apart from these stories, there is no evidence in the Gospels that the Pharisees were involved in his death. It is significant that no mention is made, in the reports of Jesus' trial, of Pharisee charges against him for Sabbath healing, although, if the Pharisees had really thought such activities worthy of the death penalty, this would have been just the time to bring forward such charges. All in all, a dispassionate reading of the Gospels suggests that Jesus' enemy was not Pharisaism, but the High Priest, the Roman appointee who regarded Jesus as a danger to Roman rule over Judaea.

Plucking corn

There appears to be one story, however, in which a conflict between Jesus and the Pharisees over Sabbath observance cannot be explained so easily. This is the story about the corn-plucking (Mark 2.23–28; Matthew 12.1–8; Luke 6.1–5). Here it is not a question of Sabbath healing, which the Pharisees, as we have seen, permitted, but of a serious infringement of Pharisee law. Jesus, it is told, allowed his disciples to pluck ears of corn on the Sabbath, and this is a plain instance of 'work' included in the list of thirty-nine prohibited activities. Surely this story shows Jesus actually abrogating the Sabbath as it was understood by the Pharisees, and declaring himself free of Pharisaic categories of thought? This is a very interesting case, which will repay investigation, as it throws light on the religious standpoint of the Pharisees, and also on the perennial question, central to the study of first-century Judaism, 'How far was Jesus an innovator in religion?' For our concept of first-century Judaism, and especially of its most progressive variety, Pharisaism, will depend on whether we consider that, in certain respects, it needed to be superseded or fulfilled by a new teaching and indeed a new religion, centred on the person and teaching of Jesus.

The Pharisees prohibited the plucking of even a few ears of corn on the Sabbath, because this was regarded as coming into the category of 'reaping', one of the prohibited kinds of 'work'. It is clear that the Bible prohibits 'work' on the Sabbath, and also that under any definition of 'work', reaping, an important agricultural activity, must be included. Jesus was not trying to abolish the Sabbath, since he describes it as a gift from God, and must therefore have accepted that reaping must not be performed on the Sabbath. A possibility to be considered, however, is that he regarded the plucking of a few ears of corn as too trivial to be considered 'reaping', and he objected to the Pharisee doctrine that even the smallest instance of 'reaping' should be classed as 'work', even if very little physical effort was involved. The incident, therefore, might be thought to be a protest against the pettiness of Pharisee definitions, and a call for a more realistic definition of 'work' in terms of palpable effort.

In general, the Pharisees did not define 'work' in terms of

physical effort. Indeed, one was permitted, in Pharisee law, to engage in considerable physical and mental effort on the Sabbath, as long as there was no infringement of the thirty-nine prohibited *kinds* of activity. Thus to detach even one plant for the purpose of eating was regarded as the *kind* of activity that was forbidden. For one day in the week, the observant Jew was to exist without disturbing the vegetable environment. This was not a petty idea, but a profoundly thoughtful one, as it was not a matter of quantity, but of principle. To object on the ground of the small quantities involved would be like regarding a vegetarian as petty because he refuses to eat even the smallest quantity of food derived from an animal. (In some contexts, however—for example, in the matter of forbidden foods—the Pharisees did consider that trivial quantities should be ignored.)

But it is much more to the point that the story, as it develops, shows clearly that Jesus was not concerned about the quantities involved. His defence of his disciples' conduct in plucking the ears of corn shows that he had other considerations in mind. Indeed, his defence puts him in line with Pharisee thought, and the story, on full inspection, turns out to have much in common with the stories about Sabbath healing already discussed.

Relevant to Jesus' defence is a significant difference between the three versions of the story found in the Synoptic Gospels. In Matthew, it is said that the disciples who plucked the corn were 'hungry', while in the other two accounts, this detail is missing. The question that needs to be asked is 'How hungry were they?'

The key-word 'hungry' occurs again in the story (in all versions) in the course of Jesus' defence of the disciples. Jesus' argument is as follows:

Have you never read what David did when he and his men were hungry and had nothing to eat? He went into the House of God, in the time of Abiathar the High Priest, and ate the consecrated loaves, though no one but a priest is allowed to eat them, and even gave them to his men.

(Mark 2.25–26)

It seems clear, then, that Jesus' disciples were indeed, as Matthew says, 'hungry', since otherwise Jesus' citation of the case of David and his men and of their hunger would not have been appropriate. And Jesus' disciples must have been very hungry indeed, if they were as hungry as David and his men, who, as Jesus is careful to point out, were not only hungry, but 'had nothing to eat'. It seems then that Jesus is not only pointing out that his disciples were hungry, but making this the main point in their defence.

A comparison with the rabbinic literature that comments on the story of David and the consecrated loaves (1 Samuel 21.6) throws further light on this defence by Jesus. The rabbis' explanation of the David incident is that David and his men were starving and thus in danger of their lives (Babylonian Talmud, Menahot 95b). For this reason the consecrated loaves, being the only food available, could be given to non-priests to eat, which would normally be strictly forbidden. Indeed, while the bread was on the golden table in the Sanctuary it was forbidden to priests too; but a starving man, whether priest or non-priest, had to be fed even if this meant taking the consecrated bread from the golden table in the Sanctuary. Jesus shows full knowledge of this Pharisee explanation of the David incident, and without this explanation his quotation of the David case makes little sense. For why, otherwise, should Jesus mention it at all? Is he simply saying, 'David rode roughshod over the laws of the Torah, and so can I?' Such an argument could hardly appeal to an audience who believed, with good reason, that David was a pious man who would not be willing to flout the sanctities of the Sanctuary unless this was warranted by special circumstances. And why does Jesus quote a case that has nothing to do with the Sabbath, to justify a breach of the Sabbath laws? But if we assume that Jesus had the Pharisee explanation of the David case in mind, the reference makes perfect sense. For it was a well-known Pharisee principle that, to save human life, all ceremonial laws should be broken, whether the laws of the Sabbath and festivals, or the laws of the sanctities of the Temple. Jesus is saying, 'Just as David ignored the Temple sanctities, being justified by the circumstances of emergency, so I am ignoring the Sabbath sanctities, being justified by the very same circumstances of emergency'.

Of course, in Mark and Luke, no sense of emergency is included in the story, and the disciples are depicted as gratuitously munching ears of corn from the field, even though they were not particularly hungry, much less starving to death. Matthew does retain some sense of emergency, but this must have been even greater in the source that the Synoptics have edited. Their motivation in editing out the emergency situation seems obvious enough: Jesus, in accordance with later Christian teaching, was to be portrayed as flouting the Torah, not as interpreting it in

48

Pharisee style. But the story, as edited, makes little sense; Jesus quotes an entirely inappropriate case from Scripture. In historical fact, Jesus was often on the run from his enemies (who were not the Pharisees, but the Romans and their Jewish henchmen, the Herodians and the Sadducees), and this may have been one such desperate occasion, when he and his disciples found themselves reduced to eating corn from a field (not a diet one would voluntarily choose). Jesus justified this, even though it was the Sabbath, by referring to the humane laws of the Pharisees, which put human need before all ceremonial laws. Further, if Jesus was on the run, this would have made his quotation of the David case even more appropriate; for it was while on the run from his deadly enemy, Saul, that David met with the same dilemma. The parallel suggests, in fact, that this incident in Jesus' life could have taken place while he was being pursued by the Galilean ruler, Herod Antipas, who sought his life just as Saul sought David's. When he was later questioned about the incident, his hostile critics were probably not the Pharisees but the Sadducees (as suggested above in relation to the Sabbath-healing stories), and he replied to them in typical Pharisee style. It should be noted that it was in connection with this same incident that Jesus is reported to have said, 'The Sabbath was made for man, not man for the Sabbath,' which, as we saw above, was a characteristic Pharisee saying used to justify the breaking of Sabbath laws in time of emergency, such as serious illness. Thus the explanation of the corn-plucking incident given here puts it in line with the Sabbath-healing stories, as having the same lesson to teach. An emergency threatening life, whether through illness or external circumstances, came under the Pharisee rubric of *piqquah nefesh* ('saving of life'), justifying the temporary abrogation of even the most important ceremonial laws until the emergency was over. If a human life was in danger, the Pharisees taught, there was no ceremonial law in Judaism that was too holy to be suspended.

It was not only ceremonial laws that had to give way to the need for saving human life. Many of the moral laws, too, the Pharisees taught, must be regarded as secondary to the duty of saving human life. Thus there was no doubt, in the mind of the Pharisees, that the laws of property were all of subsidiary importance, compared with this duty. A mother who stole food to feed a starving child was regarded as performing a meritorious act, not as committing a sin. The idea of punishing theft by capital punishment would have seemed preposterous to the Pharisees, and is indeed contrary to the plain text of the Torah even without Pharisee interpretation. The abolition of Pharisee law by the Christian Church, in the belief that Jesus had abrogated such teaching, meant the loss of many such humane legal concepts, which were recovered only after many centuries.

Indeed, the Pharisee doctrine that the need to save human life overrides the laws of property is very relevant to the consideration of the story under discussion, the corn-plucking incident. Few readers of this story stop to ask themselves the question, 'How were Jesus' disciples justified in plucking and eating corn that did not belong to them?' Quite apart from the Sabbath question that forms the kernel of the story, the theft question is one that needs to be asked. Perhaps readers unconsciously answer this question by the principle '*de minimis non curat lex*' (the law does not deal with trivialities); the farmer who owned the field would not be troubled by the loss of a few ears of corn. This hardly answers the question, however. Twelve disciples who were 'hungry' could make substantial inroads into a field of corn. Even more to the point, if it were accepted as a general principle that passers-by could help themselves to their fill of corn in a field, there would soon be nothing left. On considering the effects of universalizing such a practice, no honest person would permit himself to eat corn without the owner's permission. Perhaps, then, the owner did give his permission? Nothing in the text, however, supports such a guess. Some scholars have attempted to solve this problem by citing a passage in Deuteronomy: 'When thou comest into the standing corn of thy neighbour, then thou mayest pluck the ears with thy hand' (Deuteronomy 23.25). This apparently amazingly generous permission, however, was regarded in Pharisee tradition as referring only to labourers in a field, who were permitted to eat corn as they were working. (The Qumran sect, however, seem to have interpreted the text more literally, as giving permission to eat even to passers-by, as long as they were poor (4Q159).) On the human level, this permission for labourers was similar to the injunction in relation to animals, 'Thou shalt not muzzle the ox that treadeth out the corn' (Deuteronomy 25.4). Such humane legislation is generous enough without converting it into a *carte blanche* permission to casual passers-by to loot fields, which would make agriculture impossible.

Thus on the usual interpretation of the corn-plucking incident, as a casual Sabbath-breaking combined with a casual infringement of the laws of property, the story is inexplicable. But if the story is regarded, as argued above, as concerned with a situation of *emergency*, all becomes plain. For in an emergency involving danger to human life (in this case by starvation, as in the parallel case of David and his men), not only was it regarded as a duty to override ceremonial laws such as those of the Sabbath or the sanctities of the Temple, but also to override moral laws, such as the law of theft. A person who allowed himself to die of starvation rather than steal food was not regarded, in Pharisee thinking, as behaving admirably, but as wantonly throwing away a human life, and as guilty of the crime of suicide. This was not regarded as 'the lesser of two evils' (as in some Christian thinking on this subject), but as a matter of plain duty, where it was wrong to sacrifice the higher good to the lower.

This does not mean that the Pharisees thought that the preservation of human life was the highest of all values. There were *some* moral imperatives which they regarded as more important than life itself, for which one must be prepared to suffer death. During the first century, there was discussion among the Pharisees about which imperatives demanded this high status. It was eventually agreed that there were three: the laws against murder and against the most serious sexual offences (incest and adultery), and the prohibition of idolatry. No-one was entitled to murder another in order to save his own life, or to commit incest or adultery if ordered to do so by tyrannical authority on pain of death. Many Jews (and, of course, many Christians too) sacrificed their lives rather than perform idolatrous rites before the statues of deified emperors or other gods, and this was considered an act of the highest merit deserving the name of martyrdom.

Thus there was some limit to the flexibility of the Pharisees. Some imperatives were regarded as absolute. But in general, the Pharisees were very far from being the inflexible rigorists portrayed in the Gospels. They considered that the laws laid down in the Torah were often subject to exceptions, in accordance with circumstances. They gave much thought to the relative importance of the biblical laws, so that the lesser laws could give way to the more important ones in special circumstances, when a conflict of duties took place. It is not in the history of Pharisaic Judaism that we must look for examples of the rigoristic application of laws; for example, the punishment of starving people found guilty of theft by execution or transportation.

In accordance with their humane, flexible approach, the Pharisees enacted many great reforms and other innovations in Judaism. In the next chapter, we shall be considering these examples of Pharisee religious creativity.

4

Religious Reforms

The remark of Josephus that the Pharisees 'tend to be lenient in punishments' (*Antiquities* XIII. 10.6(294)) is certainly borne out by the Pharisee literature. We have already seen that they did not, for example, interpret the Biblical injunction, 'An eye for an eye' in a literal sense, but as a requirement for monetary compensation matching the injury inflicted. It is doubtful, however, whether this should be regarded as an innovation or reform on the part of the Pharisees, for the likelihood is that, even in biblical times, the 'eye for eye' injunction was not taken literally. If the Sadducees *did* take it literally, as seems possible, this would be in line with their policy of rejecting traditional interpretations and insisting on a crudely literal reading of the Bible text. In other words, it was the Sadducees who were the innovators (although hardly reformers) in this instance, as in many similar cases.

Where the Pharisees did institute reform in this matter was in the generosity of their interpretation of the term 'compensation'. They considered that mere compensation for the injury itself was not enough, but had to be supplemented by compensation for sufferings incidental to the injury. The Mishnah sums up as follows: 'If a man wounded his fellow, he thereby becomes liable on five counts: for injury, for pain, for healing, for loss of time, and for indignity inflicted' (Baba Kamma 8.1). The payments for loss of time and for healing (i.e. doctor's bills) are indeed biblical (see Exodus 21.19, a verse that alone is sufficient to refute the literal interpretation of 'eye for an eye'); but the payments for 'pain' and for 'indignity inflicted' are Pharisaic additions. The assessment for pain was made in this way: 'they estimate how much money such a man would be willing to take to suffer so'. The payment for 'indignity inflicted' takes into account any humiliating circumstances involved in the injury.

Capital punishment

The 'leniency' of the Pharisees can be seen especially in their attitude towards capital punishment. Though the Bible prescribes capital punishment for many offences, including Sabbath-breaking and adultery, the Pharisees were most reluctant to carry out such a punishment, and refused to do so unless the evidence of the offence was unmistakable. Thus no-one could be convicted unless there were two eye-witnesses of the actual committing of the offence. So far, this was biblical law (Numbers 35.30, Deuteronomy 17.6), but the Pharisees added further restrictions designed to ensure that there could be no doubt that the offence was committed with full intent. Thus the accused could not be convicted unless he had been *warned* by one of the witnesses not to commit the offence. Without such a warning, it was felt, the offender might not have realized quite what he was doing. Thus circumstantial evidence was entirely ruled out in all capital cases.

In one of the stories that circulated among the Pharisees, the great Simeon ben Shetach, the adviser of Queen Salome Alexandra, is said to have seen a man rushing by, with a drawn sword in his hand. Simeon followed him into a nearby house, where he found him standing over a newly killed corpse with the sword, reeking with blood, in his hand. 'Alas!' said Simeon, 'Though I am sure this man has just committed murder, it is impossible to convict him'. Some scholars have argued that the humane rules relating to capital punishment are of a date later than the lifetime of Jesus, but although the rabbinic literature that outlines these rules admittedly belongs to a later period, the rules themselves are consistently attributed to the Pharisees of Jesus' time or earlier, as in the above story about Simeon ben Shetach, who lived about a hundred years before Jesus' birth.

We must conclude, therefore, that the Pharisees depicted in the Gospels as opponents of Jesus because of his alleged offences against Jewish law are caricatures (e.g. Mark 3.6, Matthew 12.14). Not only were the alleged offences of Sabbath healing not offences at all (see chapter 3), but even if they had been *capital offences,* it would have been almost impossible to secure a conviction, given the Pharisee rules of evidence.

A well-known case in the New Testament is the 'woman taken in adultery' (John 8.3–11), where the leniency of Jesus is contrasted with the desire of the Pharisees to stone the woman to death. In fact, executions for adultery were unheard of among the Pharisees, since the kind of evidence required for conviction in such a case was, in the nature of things, impossible. But, in any case, scholars now agree that the story of the 'woman taken in adultery' is not an authentic part of the Gospel, being missing in the earliest manuscripts. The story may have been written as a piece of anti-Pharisee propaganda long after the lifetime of Jesus.

It should be noted that the Pharisees repudiated the definition of 'stoning' as meaning 'execution by throwing stones at a convicted person', and interpreted it in a different way (throwing from a height) which meant a quick death. So even in the very rare event of a capital punishment being carried out, it would not be the cruel, piecemeal death generally understood by the term 'stoning'.

Suspicion of adultery

Other Pharisee reforms softened the harshness of some of the biblical laws. For example, the Bible prescribes an ordeal for the 'woman suspected of adultery' (Numbers 5.11–31). In a solemn rite in the Temple, the woman was to drink water containing dust from the Temple floor and the ink of written curses; if she was guilty, this would cause 'her belly to swell, and her thigh to rot'. This ordeal was at least more rational than other ordeals recorded of primitive tribes and in medieval Europe, in which some positive sign of the woman's innocence was needed to clear her; in this ordeal, if nothing happened (the most likely event), the woman was cleared. Nevertheless, it was a humiliating experience for a woman to undergo, and the Pharisee teacher, Johanan ben Zakkai, a contemporary of Jesus, suspended it. The justification that he offered for this daring suspension of a plain provision of the Torah is interesting. He cited the text, 'I will not punish your daughters when they commit whoredom, nor your spouses when they commit adultery: for themselves are separated with whores, and they sacrifice with harlots' (Hosea 4.14). He deduced from this, 'If you yourselves are above reproach, the water will put your wives to the proof; otherwise it will not put them to the proof'. In other words, men were not entitled to make their wives undergo an ordeal on suspicion of adultery until men themselves could prove that they were themselves beyond suspicion of the same crime. This is a typical example of the Pharisee method of reform. A law could not be abolished in an outright manner, since it had the sanction of holy writ; but it could be nullified by an argument derived from contemporary circumstances. Johanan is saying, 'Perhaps men were righteous enough to submit their wives to such an ordeal in time gone by, but they certainly are not now'. The Pharisees' ingenious way of arguing is often condemned on the ground that it made life more complicated and burdensome. This is to overlook the many occasions when the Pharisees used their power of subtle argument to make life *less* burdensome, and to reduce the suffering that might arise from over-severe laws.

Ammonites and Moabites

Another example of the Pharisees' reforming activity may be taken from the time of Gamaliel II, who succeeded Johanan ben Zakkai as president of the academy of Jabneh (about 80 C.E.). At this time, the Mishnah relates (Yadaim 4.4), an Ammonite proselyte (convert to Judaism) applied for permission to 'enter the congregation', in apparent contradiction to the biblical injunction 'An Ammonite or a Moabite shall not enter into the congregation of the Lord' (Deuteronomy 23.3). It may be asked, 'How did this question come to be discussed, since the Ammonite in question had already been received as a proselyte, and had received the Jewish name, Judah?' It must be understood, however, that 'to enter the congregation of the Lord', in Pharisee tradition, did not mean 'to be converted to Judaism', for there were no restrictions of any kind on this. It meant 'to be accepted as a marriage partner within the Jewish community without restrictions'. Thus the biblical law forbidding Ammonites and Moabites to 'enter the congregation' for ten generations (as a punishment for their hostility to the Israelites in the Exodus period) was taken to mean that they might be accepted as converts at once, but for ten generations might marry only other similar converts, after which they might marry any Jew without restriction. The biblical law, thus understood, although it did not prevent Ammonites from becoming Jews at once, was nevertheless discriminatory, and the application by Judah was to have the marriage restriction lifted, despite its biblical authority. In this application he was successful for, after some discussion, the rabbis, following the lead of Rabbi Joshua, decided that the biblical law could be suspended. Again, an ingenious reason was found to justify the suspension. As Rabbi Joshua put it, 'Are the Ammonites and the Moabites still where they were? Long ago, Sennacherib, King of Assyria, came up and put all the nations in confusion.' The argument might be put as follows: 'In bygone days, everyone knew who was an Ammonite and who was a Moabite. But now the nations have been mixed up so much, by shiftings of population caused by military and political upheavals, that there are no pure Ammonites or Moabites left. The biblical law about them, therefore, has gone into abeyance.' Thus a much-needed reform is justified on historical grounds. The biblical law is not abolished; it no longer applies, since it referred to people who no longer exist. (For some more general remarks about the Pharisee attitude towards conversion to Judaism, see chapter 9.)

Women's rights

An important area of Pharisee reform was in matters relating to the status of women. We have seen already that one humiliating ordeal prescribed for some women by the Bible was suspended, but there were many other similar provisions—so much so that the status of women in Pharisaic Judaism (contrary to what has often been said) was far higher than that found in Christian countries until very recent times. Thus a married woman, in Pharisaic law, did not lose property rights. Any woman who brought property into her marriage, the Pharisees ruled, still owned that property, which had to be returned to her in the event of divorce. The most that a husband could claim was the profit accruing from his wife's property; he had no right whatsoever to the capital. Even this profit, however, could be claimed by the husband only if he made himself responsible for her maintenance. This was a matter for the wife to decide: if she preferred to be responsible for her maintenance herself, her husband could not claim the profit, since he was doing nothing to deserve it. On the other hand, if a woman entered marriage without any property at all of her own, she was not allowed to be at her husband's mercy in financial matters. By an enactment of the same Simon ben Shetach mentioned above (who flourished at about 100 B.C.E.), every husband was obliged to settle on his wife on marriage a substantial sum (equivalent to the provision of food and clothing for one year) which had to be paid to her in the event of divorce, or on the death of the husband. A marriage document, known as the *Ketubah*, was instituted, stating the rights of the wife in full, and this document, owned by every Jewish wife to this day, guarantees her property rights in all circumstances. It is extraordinary, then that it has so often been believed that in Pharisee law 'women had no rights', and that it was only the advent of Christianity that raised women to the status of legal personages. The historical fact is that the abolition of Pharisee law by the Church led to the loss of much humane legislation and to a tragic lowering of the status of women.

Another important aspect of women's rights is the right to divorce. This, again, is a topic on which many misunderstandings are current about Pharisaic and rabbinic law. It is often said that, in Jewish law, only a man is allowed to give a divorce, not a woman. This is technically correct, for the Bible makes provision for a man to divorce his wife (Deuteronomy 24.1), but not for a wife to divorce her husband. But again, Pharisee law was not content to accept a literal interpretation of the Bible in this matter, and rules were developed by which a woman could free herself of an intolerable marriage, while still having her property rights protected. The procedure was that a woman could bring a divorce suit in the courts and, as a result, the husband could be compelled by the court to give the wife a divorce. Thus the letter of the biblical law was preserved (since the divorce procedure consisted of the handing of a 'bill of divorcement' by the husband to the wife), but the inequality of the biblical institution was abolished. Moreover, the rights of women in this context were very liberally interpreted. A woman could sue for divorce not just on grounds of serious ill-treatment, but on grounds of incompatibility of lifestyles. Thus if a husband, against his wife's wishes, wished to change his residence from the city to the country, or vice versa, his wife was entitled to a divorce. Similarly, a man who took up a profession, such as that of a tanner, that caused him to smell badly, was compelled to release his wife from the marriage if she so wished (see Mishnah, Ketubot 7.10 and 13.10).

The Jewish attitude towards sex was much more positive and relaxed than the later Christian attitude. Either a husband or a wife could obtain a divorce if their sex life was unsatisfactory. Marriage was regarded as a contract between a man and a woman, not as an indissoluble union or sacrament. Thus if the conditions of the contract were not satisfactorily fulfilled, the marriage could be ended to avoid further misery, and a more suitable partner could be sought.

Why, then, did Jesus, a first-century Jew, condemn divorce, saying, 'Whoever divorces his wife and marries another commits adultery against her: so too, if she divorces her husband and marries another, she commits adultery' (Mark 10.11–12)? (This saying, by the way, gives valuable evidence that the wife's right to divorce, clearly stated in the Mishnah, existed in pre-Mishnaic times too in Judaism.) Jesus may have believed that the Last Days were at hand, that soon all imperfection would end and mankind would revert to the condition of Adam and Eve in the Garden of Eden before the Fall. In fact, this world of perfection did not arrive. Christians, however, attempted to implement Jesus' saying in a kind of world for which it might never have been intended.

The position of women in first-century Judaism was far from perfect. Women were confined, on the whole, to the home, where, however, they had much religious responsibility. Few women played a role in the larger world of the synagogue and the academy (but see chapter 5). In a society in which large families were the rule, this was inevitable. However, respect for women was guaranteed by the Fifth Commandment, which made honouring one's mother just as important as honouring one's father. Moreover, the Bible held up many models of revered women: the four Matriarchs, Sarah, Rebekah, Leah and Rachel; the prophetesses Miriam, Deborah and Hulda; the saviour Esther; and Ruth the exemplar of loyalty and true conversion to Judaism. The rabbis stressed the honour due to a wife. One saying is: 'He who has no wife lives without good or help or joy or blessing or atonement' (Genesis Rabbah XVII. 2). Another is: 'Be careful about the honour of your wife, for blessing enters the house only because of the wife' (b. Baba Metzia 59a).

5

The Synagogue

Both the literary sources and modern archaeological research attest that wherever there were Jews, there were synagogues, which functioned as houses of both prayer and study. The significance of the synagogue in Jewish religion of the first century cannot be overestimated.

Synagogue and temple

The synagogue was a local centre, serving the needs of the local population throughout Palestine and the Diaspora. The meaning of the word 'synagogue' is simply 'meeting', and it is a Greek translation of the Hebrew expression bet ha-keneset, meaning 'house of assembly'. The synagogue has never been, and is not today, a place where religious sacraments are performed. It is not presided over by priests, nor are any mystical rites performed in it. It is essentially a place where people meet to pray together and to study together. It must therefore be distinguished from the religious centres, known as 'shrines' or 'temples', that operated in the other religions of the ancient world. In these, an individual entered to conduct a sacrificial rite together with a priest. In early Judaism, as the Bible attests, local shrines existed as in other religions; but by the reforms described in the Book of Deuteronomy, all these local shrines were abolished (in the seventh century B.C.E.) and only one temple was allowed, that in Jerusalem, where alone sacrifices were offered.

The synagogue arose to fill the vacuum left by the local shrine but, once it came into being, it expressed a new and original attitude to religious worship. At first, as we learn from the rabbinic literature, the synagogue was still tied to the idea of temple ritual. So that local areas should feel that they had some share in the activities of the Temple in Jerusalem, a group of laymen (known as ma'amad or 'post') would accompany the priests of the locality when it was the turn for their 'course' to officiate in the Temple. The priests (kohanim) were the descendants of Aaron. They were divided into 24 'courses' (*mishmarot*), according to their descent, each of which served in the Temple in turn for one week. For details of the 'courses' see 1 Chronicles 24.7–19 and Mishnah, Sukkah 5.6–8 (see also Luke 1.5). For the relationship between the 'course' and the *ma'amad*, see Mishnah, Ta'anit 4.2.

While the 'course' performed the daily sacrifices, the 'post' of laymen would hold a prayer meeting in the synagogue which was situated in the Temple grounds. Simultaneously, back at home, a group of laymen held a similar prayer meeting at the local synagogue. Thus the practice of lay worship acted out symbolically, and with the accompaniment of devotion of the heart, the acts of tribute to God performed by the priests in the Temple. But as time went on, the synagogue achieved greater independence from the Temple worship, and developed an ethos and atmosphere of its own.

Organization

In particular, the development of the synagogue was influenced by its democratic constitution. Since it was conceived from the first as having a representative function (being based on the elected members of the *ma'amad*, representing the entire laity of a particular locality), it was organized on the basis of elections and has remained until the present day in the hands of a lay management elected for a fixed term. The 'President' of the synagogue was thus a layman, who was in charge of its day-to-day running. The prayer services would be conducted by laymen. If a priest were present at a service, he would worship just like any other member of the congregation, except that he would be called first to the reading of the Law (see below), and at festival time he would come forward at a certain point in the service to pronounce the biblical priestly blessing, 'The Lord bless thee and keep thee. The Lord make his face shine upon thee, and be gracious unto thee. The Lord lift up his countenance upon thee, and give thee peace' (Numbers 6.24–26). This blessing, like so much else in the Jewish liturgy, was later included in the Christian order of service.

There are some interesting references to the synagogue in the New Testament, confirming details found in the rabbinic writings, and sometimes even giving details not known from any other literary source. For example, Jairus (Luke 8.41) is described as 'a ruler of the synagogue' (Greek, *archon tes synagoges*). Crispus (Acts 18.8) is called *archisynagogos*, a title found in inscriptions in excavated synagogues of the first century. The 'ruler' did not have dictatorial power in the synagogue, but had to consult another official called the 'minister' (Hebrew, *segan*, see Mishnah, Sotah 7.8), and also a committee or council of elders. There is a reference, although an unsympathetic one, to these synagogue councils in Matthew 10.17.

It is interesting that office in the synagogue was not confined to men. Some excavated inscriptions describe certain women as '*archisynagogissa*' ('head of synagogue') and *presbytera* ('elder' or 'member of council'). Some scholars argue that these were only honorary titles, but even so they show that great honour was paid to women in the synagogues. During the first century, the synagogues actually gave more equal treatment to women than in later centuries, when women were seated separately from men and the women's seating section was divided off by a partition. Also, there is evidence that women took a larger part in the actual service in the first century than in later times. A growth in prudishness and concern for decorum led to these changes in the synagogue, as they did in the Christian churches, where the role of women was also much reduced in a short space of time (see 1 Corinthians 14.34–35). But at the time when Paul directed that women's voices should not be heard in church, the position of women had not yet deteriorated in the synagogue. Paul's demotion of women was, therefore, not a consequence of his Pharisee background.

There is also evidence in the New Testament that the membership of a synagogue did not always depend on sharing the same locality, but might derive from certain interests or associations held in common. Thus the New Testament refers to a 'Synagogue of Freedmen' (Acts 6.9), the members of which had been in captivity and slavery together. Other synagogues in Jerusalem were for the use of people of certain localities outside Palestine (Cyrenians, Alexandrians, Cilicians) when they came up to Jerusalem for the festivals, or to take up permanent residence there. Even today, there are synagogues of this sort in Jerusalem, catering for people who come from the same town in Poland or Russia. One of the synagogues in Jerusalem was that of the Nazarenes, who had in common their belief in the Messiahship of Jesus. This Nazarene synagogue is not really correctly named 'the Jerusalem Church', as it remained attached to Judaism in every way (allegiance to the Temple, practice of circumcision, observance of the Jewish Sabbath and festivals, etc.).

Throughout the Jewish Diaspora, the synagogue was the institution that provided cohesion and continuity. A big city would contain not one but many synagogues. Some were very humble, being no more than a meeting place in the home of one of the members. Some were magnificent buildings. The greatest was in Alexandria, where it was said that signals had to be given to worshippers to indicate to them when to say 'Amen', since the reader was too far away to be audible. The synagogue was all-important in preserving Judaism in the Diaspora, because of the remoteness of the Temple. Philo attests, 'On the Sabbath days in all the cities thousands of houses of learning were opened, in which discernment and moderation and proficiency and righteous living and indeed all virtues were taught' (*De spec. leg.* II. 15(62)). Paul, on his journeys, found Jewish synagogues wherever he went.

Pharisee influences

Liturgy

In all the synagogues, during the first century, the dominant influence was that of the Pharisees. This is shown particularly in the liturgy created by the Pharisees which was in general use in the synagogues.

The Jewish liturgy at the present day contains many elements that were added in later centuries, but its main outline was complete even in the first century.[1] It consisted of the recitation of the *Shema'*, the affirmation of the unity of God, and also of the *Tephillah*, or 'prayer', consisting of blessings and petitions.

The word *Shema'* means 'Hear', which is the first word of the two biblical sentences that form the centre of the Pharisee liturgy:

> 'Hear O Israel, the Lord our God is one Lord. And thou shalt love the Lord with all thy heart, with all thy soul and with all thy might.'

> (Deuteronomy 6.4–5)

Jesus too stressed these verses as of paramount importance (Mark 12.29–30).) The blessings accompanying this recital

[1] For the liturgy see S. Singer, *The Authorized Daily Prayer Book*. Eyre and Spottiswoode, 1918.

stress God's role as Creator and as loving Father. In the 'blessings' (*berakhot*) of the liturgy, the innermost feelings and religious concepts of the Pharisee sages are particularly to be found: love of God and man; the religious mission of Israel as a priest-nation working for the messianic kingdom of God; the coming era of peace and justice; the resurrection of the dead. Their system of values is shown also in the selection they made from the biblical Psalms and other biblical works for inclusion in the liturgy, particularly the succession of psalms that was called the *Hallel*, recited on festivals (Psalms 113–18).

The Sages also created a pattern of worship for the home. They composed the blessings of the *Kiddush* ('sanctification') ceremony performed by the head of the household with wine at the beginning of a Sabbath or festival meal, and also the blessings of Grace, recited after every meal containing bread, even during weekdays. The most impressive domestic rite was the Passover *Seder*, with its special rubric, the *Haggadah* (see section on story-telling below).

Certain other observances were characteristic of Pharisee worship. Phylacteries (*tephillin*) were worn during prayer and also fringes on the corners of garments, in accordance with biblical commands. Also, the *mezuzah*, a little box containing the *Shemaʿ* was attached to the doorpost of the house, again in fulfilment of a biblical command. These observances, as the Bible says, were intended to promote continual awareness of the unity of God. (For the biblical origins of phylacteries, fringes and the *mezuzah*, see Deuteronomy 6.8, Numbers 15.37–40 and Deuteronomy 6.9, respectively. Phylacteries and fringes are both mentioned in Matthew 23.5, and the wearing of fringes is possibly referred to by Jesus in Matthew 9.20.)

The role of the rabbi

The Pharisee sages themselves performed a special role in the synagogue. This was to act as teachers, advisers and consultants. They had no priestly role, and took part in the services as ordinary worshippers, not as officiants, although, in reverence to them, the congregation usually allotted them a special seat near the side of the synagogue facing Jerusalem (see Matthew 23.6 for an unsympathetic reference to this). Each synagogue, if possible, had its own resident sage or rabbi (though this title was not current until the latter part of the first century). Members of the congregation would go to the sage with their problems, whether personal or religious, and he would act as judge or arbitrator where differences between members arose. He was not a paid official even in these capacities, for the Pharisees disapproved of taking a salary for acting as a sage, which they called 'using the Torah as a spade to dig with'. It was only at a much later period of Judaism, in the Middle Ages, when times were harder, that it became usual to pay a rabbi a salary. Even as late as the twelfth century, the famous rabbi Maimonides refused to accept payment for his heavy and devoted rabbinical duties, and instead made his living as a physician. Various rabbinic sayings underline this reluctance to turn the rabbinate into a salaried profession: for example, 'It is better for a man to skin animal carcases than to say to the community, 'Support me, I am a great sage' (Baba Batra 110a). This feeling is in the background of Paul's remarks on this issue (1 Corinthians 9.4–15), in which he defends the right of the apostles to be supported by the community, yet remarks that he himself has never availed himself of this right. It is interesting that Paul uses the example of the priests to vindicate the right of the apostles to payment. But this, in fact, is a parallel that the rabbis never used, for the whole point was that they, the rabbis, were not priests, but essentially laymen, whose work was within the community.

The use of parables

One of the most important contributions of the Pharisees to the life of the synagogue was the sermon. This discourse, taking place on Sabbaths and festivals, was a characteristic creation of Pharisaism. In it, the underlying emotion and idealism of Pharisaic Judaism were given expression in a form that was readily understood even by the humblest of the people. A Pharisee sage had to be an expert in law, so that he could act as judge in legal cases brought before him; but he also had to keep in touch with the moral attitudes and emotional impulses underlying the formulations of the law. In the sermon, he could lay aside the intricacies of legal argument and speak to people's hearts; and this he could do best by having recourse to the story element in Judaism. In the Bible, there are both laws and stories, and especially there is the basic story on which Judaism is based, that of the Exodus: how God led out an enslaved nation into the desert, and there made them into a nation of free people, so that he could then give them the Promised Land, in which a new kind of society was to be slowly and painfully realized—a society based on values of love of neighbour, justice, equality and peace. The great chain of stories in the Hebrew Bible was the subject matter of the Pharisee sermon, but the preacher was also himself a story-maker. It was in these sermons that the parable first became a regularly-used technique for the conveying of religious truths.

Jesus' use of parables stamps him as a teacher of the rabbinic kind. It is significant that the Gospel of John, which gives a very different picture of Jesus from that found in the other Gospels, does not contain a single parable. It is the Synoptic Gospels, which preserve many other Jewish characteristics of Jesus, that contain Jesus' parables. Many parallels can be found in the rabbinic writings to the parables of Jesus—indeed, the rabbinic sources often throw light on the original form of a New Testament parable that has been overlaid by ideas deriving from a period later than that of Jesus.

For example, here is a typical Pharisee parable:

A certain king had a garden, in which were planted rows of fig trees, vines, pomegranates and apples. He entrusted it to a tenant-farmer and went away. After a time, the king returned, and looking into the garden to know what it had produced, found it full of thorns and thistles. So he brought in woodcutters to destroy the garden utterly. But as he looked among the thorns, he noticed a single rose-coloured flower. He took it, and smelt it, and his spirit found rest in it. Said the king, 'For the sake of this flower, the whole garden will be saved'.

(Midrash, Leviticus Rabbah 23.3)

The narrative elements of king and servants, or landlord and tenant-farmer, appear again and again in the rabbinic parables, as in those of Jesus, always symbolizing the relation between God and man, and God's forgiveness and mercy.

Another Pharisee parable exphasizes God's love for the convert, who has made great sacrifices to join God's people:

A king had a flock, which went out to the fields, and came in again in the evening. So it was every day. One day a stag came in with the flock. He went along with the goats and grazed with them. The king was told, 'A stag has joined the flock and is grazing with them every day, going out with them and coming in with them'. The king felt love for the stag, and when he saw him going out to the fields, he gave orders, 'Let him have good pasture according to his will: no man shall beat him; take great care with him!' And also when the stag came in with the flock, the king would say, 'Give him to drink'. So he showed that he loved him very much. The king's servants said to him, 'My lord, how many rams are yours, how many sheep are yours, how many goats are yours, yet you give us no special instructions concerning them. Yet about this stag, every day, you give us your commands.' Said the king to them, 'The flock, whether they want to or not, thus is their way, to graze in the field every day, and in the evening to come in to sleep in the fold. The stags sleep in the wilderness; it is not their way to enter the places cultivated by men. Shall we not account it as a merit to this one who has left behind the whole of the broad, vast wilderness, the abode of all the beasts, and has come to stay in the courtyard?' So God has told us, 'Love ye therefore the proselyte' (Deuteronomy 10.19).

(Midrash, Numbers Rabbah 8.2)

The concern for the convert to Judaism shown in this parable arises from the universalistic spirit of the Pharisees, to which even the New Testament attests, though unsympathetically, when it says of the Pharisees, '... ye compass sea and land to make one proselyte...' (Matthew 23.15). (For further treatment of Pharisee universalism, see chapter 9.)

The aim of the rabbinic use of the parable is always to make the religious themes more simple and vivid, so that they could be more easily understood and assimilated by the ordinary people. Unfortunately, however, at a later stage after Jesus' death, the idea arose that his parables were intended as *riddles* by which he wished to exclude the mass of the people from understanding his message (Luke 8.10, Mark 4.11, Matthew 13.13). This idea arose at a time when Jesus was being portrayed as estranged from the Jewish people, who were doomed to be rejected by God in favour of the Gentiles.

The parables of the Pharisee sages and their successors, the rabbis, are found chiefly in the type of work known as *Midrash* (plural, *Midrashim*), which began to be written down in the third century C.E. although their content had been transmitted orally for a long time before that. The earlier Midrashim (Mekilta, Sifra and Sifre) consist of consecutive commentary on the Pentateuch, but the later Midrashim, known as the Homiletic Midrashim, are in the form of sermons, or sermonic material, based on the main preaching occasions of the religious year and on the texts used in the synagogue readings from the Bible on

those occasions. Some Christian scholars, anxious to preserve a belief in the originality of Jesus, have denied that any of this Midrashic material can be regarded as earlier than, or contemporary with, the time of Jesus. According to this view, the parables
ound in the Midrashim derive from those of Jesus. This view, however, is most implausible for many reasons (one of which has been mentioned already, the fact that the Midrashic form of a parable is sometimes clearly earlier than that found in a Gospel). In any case, the use of parables can be found in the Bible itself: the most moving one is that told by the prophet Nathan to King David (2 Samuel 12), by which David was brought to repentance for his sin with Bathsheba.

Here is a parable about the sin of David, from the Midrash called the Sifre, which comments on the book of Deuteronomy. This parable points a moral not to be found in the New Testament, but typical of Pharisaic Judaism.

> David said to God, 'I have sinned, but let it not be written in the Bible'. God replied, 'Is it not acceptable to you that people should say, "Because he loved him, he forgave him"?' It may be likened to someone who borrowed from the king a thousand measures of wheat every year. The people used to say, 'Does he really pay back such a large amount every year? Or does the king forgive him?' One year the man failed to pay the king back. The king then took his sons and daughters and placed them on the selling-stone. In that hour, all knew that previously he had never failed to repay his debt.

David is adjured by God, in this remarkable Midrashic dialogue, to accept his role in the Bible as an example to all mankind of the power of repentance and of the mercy of the forgiving love of God, even though this means that the baseness of David's sin will be made known to all future generations. The parable that follows has the moral that those whom God especially loves should not expect their sins to be overlooked, but that, on the contrary, their sins will receive especially severe punishment (see Proverbs 3.12, 'For whom the Lord loveth he correcteth; even as a father the son in whom he delighteth'). Thus the display of the sins of the Jews and of their punishment in the Hebrew Bible should be regarded not as a sign that God has rejected the Jews (as the New Testament argues, Matthew 23.34–35, Acts 7.51–53), but as a sign of his special love for them. God forgives easily only those of whom he expects little.

The Pharisee parables sometimes have a demanding moral, by which the theme of God's forgiveness is deepened in the light of the theme of vocation.

Story-telling

The parables found in Pharisee preaching are only one example of the importance of story-telling in Pharisee religious instruction. Indeed, it would not be too much to say that story-telling fills much of the space in Pharisaic Judaism that, in Christianity, is filled by theology. This is why the non-legal part of rabbinic Judaism is given the name *haggadah* (or *aggadah*), which means literally, 'telling'. The legal aspect on the other hand, is called *halakhah*, which means literally, 'going'. The religious life, therefore, consists partly of 'telling' and partly of 'going'. The 'commandments' (*mitzvot*) of the Torah are the basic demands that are expanded, refined and adapted to ongoing life by the *halakhah*, which is the rabbinical system of laws for community living. The stories of the Bible proliferate into the multifarious story-telling of the rabbis, by which the fundamentals of Judaism are expressed in poetic narrative form. Through these stories, certain quasi-theological concepts are crystallized: concepts such as repentance, vocation, the 'kingdom of God', the messianic age, the Covenant. But these concepts do not form a systematic theology, with each concept subordinated in a total scheme. They overlap, and have shifting outlines. Some appear to conflict with others, but in the realm of poetry this does not matter, for in this realm opposing concepts complement each other. Only in the realm of *halakhah* is there a strenuous striving for consistency and decision-making, for this is the sphere of action, where decisions are urgent; not to decide is itself a decision, and probably a bad one.

On one important occasion in the Jewish year, story-telling becomes not just a mode of preaching but a religious duty. This is the occasion of the Passover, when it is the duty of every father to tell his children the story of the Exodus from Egypt. The Bible itself lays down this duty: 'And it shall be when thy son asketh thee in time to come, saying, What is this? that thou shalt say unto him, By strength of hand the Lord brought us out from Egypt, from the house of bondage' (Exodus 13.14). On the evening of Passover this duty is still performed; the liturgy of this evening service, held in the home, was composed by the Pharisees, and is called the Haggadah, or 'telling'. This specialized use of the word Haggadah should not be confused with the more generalized use of the word *haggadah* to mean the whole story-telling aspect of the Oral Torah; yet in fact the Passover Haggadah is the basic instance of this aspect. In a passage included in the Passover liturgy we are told, 'Even if we were all sages, discerning elders in the knowledge of the Law, it would still be our duty to relate the story of the Exodus from Egypt tonight'. No-one is to be regarded as above the simple duty of telling the story of the Exodus: no profound programme of research is to have precedence over this duty. For the story of the Exodus is the basis of the whole Torah, whether written or oral, in all its subtleties and ramifications; because the Torah is essentially a law of freedom, the constitution of a form of society set up by a band of escaped slaves determined to implement a vision of a society different from the slave state they had left behind them, a society in which each person would have direct access to God, unmediated by political or religious aristocracies or hierarchies. Thus the Haggadah also declares, 'In every generation each individual is obliged to regard himself as if he personally had gone forth from Egypt, as it is said, "This is done because of that which the Lord did unto me when I came forth out of Egypt" (Exodus 13.8)'. The telling of the story is what makes vivid to each person the foundation of his faith, which is rooted not in abstract theological concepts but in a cataclysmic intervention of God in human history, after which nothing was ever the same.

The Pharisee preacher, whose pulpit was in the synagogue, thus had the task of bringing to life the fundamental story of the Exodus and all the other stories which, proliferating from it, made the Hebrew Bible a texture of narrative conveying every kind of human emotion. Yet the typical Pharisee sermon, while chiefly based on *haggadah*, always had a stiffening element of *halakhah* too; for inspiration and comfort were not to remain mere emotional refreshment, but were to prompt action in the world, where the duties of being a member of human society required hard legal thought and study.

6

Religion and Education

The Pharisee sermon, described in chapter 5, was only one of the ways in which the Pharisee teachers spread knowledge of Judaism. The sermon, in fact, was the least demanding of their methods, the one that most combined entertainment with instruction. The story is told of the great Rabbi Akiba, who was born probably around 40 C.E. and died as a martyr in 137 C.E., that he once said abruptly in the course of a sermon, 'One woman in Egypt gave birth to 600 000 sons in one birth'. This occasioned great surprise, so he went on to explain that the woman concerned was Jochebed, the mother of Moses, and she did not really give birth to such a host, but only to one son, Moses, whose merit was so great that he equalled all the other Israelites put together, numbering 600 000. When asked later why he had expressed himself with such startling exaggeration, Rabbi Akiba replied, 'I noticed that some of the congregation were falling asleep, so I decided to wake them up'. This story (as well as pointing to a perennial problem faced by preachers) tells us something about Pharisee methods of Bible interpretation and explanation; playful attention-gaining devices were not to be despised if people's souls could thus be stimulated to identify with the historical mission of Israel.

Bible readings

The synagogue, however, was also a centre for more formal teaching, so that it often performed the function of *bet ha-midrash* ('house of learning') as well as that of *bet ha-keneset* ('house of meeting'). One element of instruction was built into every Sabbath and festival service: the readings from the Bible. There was a cycle of readings from the Pentateuch, so that the whole Pentateuch was read in the course of three years (later this was changed to a lectionary cycle of one year). In addition, a portion would be read from the Prophets, chosen for its relevance to the Torah (Pentateuch) portion of the week. These readings would be undertaken by members of the congregation, who would say a blessing before and after each reading, thanking God for having given the Torah to his people. In the first century, many of the audience were not capable of understanding Hebrew, so it was customary for an appointed person to accompany the reading with a translation into Aramaic, the language of the people. This Aramaic translation became standardized and was eventually written down in what was called the Targum, which has been preserved in various versions. This is a valuable source for the study of first-century Judaism, since every translation is also a commentary containing the ideas of the translator.

There is some interesting evidence in the New Testament of this practice of Bible readings in the synagogue. When Paul and his companions arrived in Pisidian Antioch, they 'went into the synagogue on the Sabbath day, and sat down. And after the reading of the law and the prophets the rulers of the synagogue sent unto them, saying, Ye men and brethren, if ye have any word of exhortation for the people, say on' (Acts 13.14–15). Here we have the reading from the Pentateuch ('the law'), the reading from the prophets, and the sermon, which could be given by a distinguished visitor, on the invitation of the lay officials, the President or the Minister. Jesus himself, when in the synagogue at Nazareth, 'stood up for to read. And there was delivered unto him the book of the prophet Esaias' (Luke 4.16–17). He read a passage from Isaiah 61, and, after closing the book, followed up his reading by preaching on the text which he had read. Here there is no mention of the previous reading from the Torah; nor is it stated that Jesus preached by invitation; nor is it clear whether Jesus read an appointed passage from the Prophets or one he chose himself (practice in this matter may have been more flexible than in later times). But at any rate, the choice of the book of Isaiah was not his, apparently, so he was following a set programme to some extent, and we can discern here the usual agenda of a Sabbath morning service, as developed by the Pharisees.

The regular readings from the Bible during services, together with translations into the vernacular, were only the minimum requirements of the Pharisee educational programme. Even the sermons hardly counted as education, since they were 'exhortations' rather than lessons. The synagogue too was where the educational programme proper began with regular lessons for the children, in which they were taught first the Torah, then the Prophets and other biblical writings, and finally the outlines of the Oral Torah. The Pharisees, indeed, instituted a programme of universal education, perhaps the earliest in history. They invested the teaching of children with a mystical aura, saying that the voices of the children in the synagogues, reciting their lessons, protected the whole nation from harm. Teachers of children were appointed in every locality, and rules were laid down; that no teacher should have a class of more than twenty-five children, for example. All this, of course, was based on the counsel of the Torah itself, which insists that the teaching of God's law should be given to every child, not to a privileged minority: 'And thou shalt teach them diligently unto thy children, and shalt talk of them when thou sittest in thine house, and when thou walkest by the way, and when thou liest down, and when thou risest up' (Deuteronomy 6.7).

Rabbinical training

A more advanced educational programme was administered by the Pharisee sages themselves for older students who wished to become sages. Sometimes these advanced classes took place in the synagogue, or a special room attached to it. Sometimes they took place in a special hall, or in the open air. These classes revolved very much round the personality of the teaching sage, who had a relationship of master and disciple with his students, rather than of teacher and pupil. A student would study the personality of his teacher, as well as listening to his formal lessons. The life of study was a dedicated one that might involve considerable sacrifice. It is described in the Mishnah as follows: 'This is the way of the Law. Thou shalt eat bread with salt and thou shalt drink water by measure, and on the ground shalt thou sleep and thou shalt live a life of trouble while thou toilest in the Law' (Mishnah, Abot 6.4). Many stories are told about the hardships suffered by famous scholars such as Hillel, Rabbi Eliezer and Rabbi Akiba while toiling to achieve knowledge.

Learning the Law

The subject matter of the formal classes was the Oral Torah, both in its aspect of *halakhah* and of *haggadah*. It was the *halakhah* that demanded hard toil especially, for here the student was expected to commit all he learned to memory. During the first century, halakhic material was just beginning to be put into writing. There were some inhibitions about doing this, not because there was any mystic idea that the Oral Torah must always remain oral, but because it was feared that compilations of Oral Torah, if widely published, might be regarded by some people as holy, inspired writings worthy to be included in the canon of the Bible, and the Pharisees were firmly of the opinion that prophetic inspiration had ceased, and the canon of the Bible was now closed. During the first century, works were still being written in other Jewish sects that aspired to be included in the Bible: for example, the apocalyptic writings which are now labelled Pseudepigrapha and some of the writings of the Qumran sect (see chapter 2). Even among the Pharisees, there was still some doubt about whether certain books should be included in the Bible; for example, debates have been recorded between Rabbi Akiba and other rabbis whether the Song of Songs should be included (Rabbi Akiba was strongly in favour of it, saying, 'All the Writings are holy, but the Song of Songs is Holy of Holies'). Other disputed books were Ecclesiastes (finally included) and the book of Ben Sira, or Ecclesiasticus (finally excluded). This delicate situation of the closing of the canon explains the rabbinic reluctance during this period to publish widely any collections that were made of Oral Torah, though these might be circulated among the students of a rabbi who had made such a compilation. In the second and third centuries, when the canon of the Bible was secure, this inhibition was lifted, and great compilations of Oral Torah appeared, including the Mishnah, Tosefta and Mekhilta, which were widely circulated, and achieved a kind of semi-canonical status that did not compete in any way with the canonicity of the Bible.

Even at that stage, however, when vast and comprehensive handbooks of Oral Torah existed, the emphasis in rabbinic training, in its halakhic aspect, remained on memorizing. There were, during the third century and later, many who knew the whole Mishnah by heart, and this kind of massive memorizing has continued in Jewish academies down to the present day. In the first century, memorizing was even more important, in the absence of any standard textbooks, even though some written aids did exist. Some modern scholars have had mistaken ideas about this phenomenon. They have likened the rabbinic memorizing to that found in primal societies, where a huge tribal lay may be known by heart by professional bards. But first-century Jewry was not a pre-literate society. On the contrary, it was highly literate, with a programme of universal literacy centred on the study of a written text, the Bible. The real parallel is with the extensive memorizing done, even in our modern society, by medical and law students. Where a large and complicated body of knowledge is needed for a practical end, often in situations of emergency in which time would be wasted by much consulting of books, memorizing will always be prized. The rabbinic students, after their training was complete, would be required to act as judges in complicated matters, and would often be consulted on personal and social matters where a knowledge of precedents and varying views was important. There were thus good practical reasons for memorizing legal topics, especially when there were no retrieval systems such as we now take for granted; concordances, indexes and computers, for example.

It should be remembered that the status of law, as a subject of study, was far higher in Judaism, and especially in Pharisaic Judaism, than in modern societies, where law is regarded as a secular subject, studied mainly for professional advancement. Judaism is to an important extent a revealed law, and to study this law was regarded as a religious duty, not merely for experts, but for everybody. Judaism has always considered that moral precepts, however true or edifying, are insufficient. The Hebrew Bible contains many such precepts, such as 'Thou shalt love thy neighbour as thyself' (Leviticus 19.18) or 'Justice, justice shalt thou pursue' (Deuteronomy 16.20), which have proved in-spiring but which do not help us to translate our good intentions into action in the complex muddle of life. This can be done only by hard thought about the actual difficulties that occur, and this process of thought issues in law. Thus the Bible tells us, 'Thou shalt not steal', and this is an important moral principle. But it leaves a multitude of questions unanswered. For example, is a mother guilty of a crime if she steals to feed a starving child? Should there be a heavier penalty for kidnapping than for stealing property? Is it theft to pocket some lost property that one happens to come across?

Or take the commandment, 'Thou shalt not kill'. Does this mean that one must not kill even in self-defence, or to save someone from being murdered? Is someone who brings about a death through an agent guilty of murder? The answers to some of these questions can be found explicitly in the Bible, but mostly such questions belong to the Oral Torah, which has asked and answered them in the course of many centuries of practical implementation of biblical principles. Some people, such as the Sadducees, thought that the building-up of precedents and rules about such questions detracted from the God-given simplicity of the Written Torah. Such a view is also found in the New

Testament, where Jesus is represented as complaining that the Pharisees were 'making the word of God of none effect through your tradition' (Mark 7.13). This complaint, if it were genuinely that of Jesus, would make him into a Sadducee, insisting that the 'word of God' (i.e. the Bible) should not be interpreted in the light of traditional qualifications and amplifications. This would mean, for example, a rigidly literal interpretation of 'an eye for an eye', and great lack of flexibility in the interpretation of laws of theft, murder etc. The point is that 'tradition' makes for greater flexibility, not less, for it takes into account many different situations that have occurred in the course of time since the giving of the Written Law. But there is no real reason to conclude that Jesus took this Sadducee position; for the passage in which the saying occurs is not authentic, as it ascribes a view to the Pharisees (about regarding vows to the Temple as more important than honour to parents) that is the exact reverse of the view they actually held.

The Seven Middot

The main study of the Pharisee academies was thus the Oral Torah, and the most strenuous part of the course was the legal aspect, the *halakhah*, which involved years of study and demanded high powers of intellect and memory. There are certain points, however, that need to be made about this, to avoid misunderstandings.

First, it should not be thought that the study of the Bible itself was neglected in the academies. On the contrary, it is clear that the Pharisee sages had intimate acquaintance with the whole Hebrew Bible, which was at their fingertips. The prophetic books of the Bible were just as familiar to them as the legal parts of the Pentateuch, and they constantly made use of prophetic passages in their sermons. The Pharisees, indeed, regarded themselves as the successors of the biblical prophets, not in the sense of being prophets themselves, but in that they had the task of interpreting the words of the prophets (often obscure and vague) and implementing their insights in the everyday life of the community. But even in their legal activity the Pharisees were not content to refer simply to tradition, or to their own legal judgments, when they expanded the words of the Bible. They were also much concerned to show that the Bible itself, if subtly interpreted, could be shown to give support to the tradition. To this end, they developed a system of hermeneutics, that is, rules by which the legal portions of the Bible could be made to yield logical conclusions in legal cases with which the Bible does not deal explicitly. This was, in a sense, the Pharisee reply to the Sadducees: to say that the 'word of God', far from being simple, was actually full of hidden subtleties that justified the Pharisee amplifications. Thus many of the Pharisee 'traditions' were justified by being traced to the text of the Bible itself. This did not really mean that the 'traditions' were held to derive their authority from such subtle exegesis, but only that it was a godly exercise to probe the mind of God in his Word, and show that it was full of hidden depths and that, simple as it might appear on the surface, it actually covered all kinds of possibilities and problems that were to appear in the course of the centuries after the revelation.

The earliest known list of these hermeneutic rules is that ascribed to the great Pharisee sage, Hillel, whose old age coincided with Jesus' youth. Hillel's list is known as the Seven *Middot* ('measures' or 'methods') and runs as follows:

1. *a fortiori* (*qal wahomer*);
2. verbal similarity (*gezerah shawah*);
3. induction (*binyan ab*);
4. 'two verses' (*sheney ketubim*);
5. the general and the particular (*kelal uperat*);
6. the particular and the general (*perat ukelal*);
7. 'something that is understood through its context' (*dabar halamed me'inyano*).

Of these seven rules, four (rules 1, 3, 5 and 6) are rules of logic, whereas the other three are rules of literary style. The assumption behind all the rules is that the Bible is both logical and stylistically subtle. Thus if the Bible makes a statement, it also means to assert everything that follows logically from that statement. Also, by the use of stylistic devices, such as repetition of a distinctive phrase, the Bible links together topics that might otherwise be regarded as unconnected. A full exposition of the seven rules would be out of place here, but some examples follow.

Rule 1 says that if a statement is made in the Bible about something 'light', then the same statement applies 'all the more so' to something 'heavy'. For example, the Bible says (Exodus 22.14) that a borrower must pay the value of a borrowed article to the owner if it becomes destroyed. But what if the article is stolen? Scripture does not tell us, but a *qal wa-homer* argument yields the answer by analogy with the case of a paid guardian:

1. a paid guardian is free from payment if the article is destroyed, but liable if it is stolen (Exodus 22.10–12);

2. therefore *all the more so*, a borrower, who is liable if the article is destroyed, should be liable if it is stolen.

It is first proved that a paid guardian is 'light' and a borrower 'heavy', and then the 'all the more so' argument is applied.

It is an important principle (known as *dayo*, literally 'it is enough for it') that the argument cannot go further than 'all the more so'. Thus the following would be an invalid *qal wa-homer* argument:

1. a moderately good child should be given a sweet;
2. therefore, a very good child should be given two sweets.

The correct conclusion is:

2. therefore *all the more so* a very good child should be given a sweet.

The latter is as far as we can go in strict logic, since any attempt to add to the information given must be arbitrary.

A biblical source was found for the *qal wa-homer* argument and for the rule of *dayo* in the story of Miriam (Numbers 12.14).

The rabbinic theory of the *qal wa-homer* argument has many other complexities, covering possible refutations of such an argument.

Rule 2 means that a distinctive phrase used in two different contexts can be taken to mean that there are legal similarities between the two contexts even though this is not explicitly stated. For example, the phrase '... that he has not stretched out his hand...' used in both Exodus 22.8 and 22.11, means that the oath required for a paid guardian in Exodus 22.11 is also required in the case of an unpaid guardian referred to in Exodus 22.8.

Rule 3 means that a general rule may be built up from two or more particular cases. For example, Exodus 21.26–27 says that freedom must be given to a slave if his master knocks out either his eye or his tooth. This was extended to the general rule, 'freedom is given for the loss of any organ'. Many logical rules were laid down for the building of such a generalization, and the resultant theory is very similar to that of 'induction' in Western logic of science, by which rules are given for the transition from particular scientific observations to the formulation of a scientific law.

Rule 4 says that two biblical verses that appear to contradict each other may be harmonized by the discovery of a third verse that reconciles the contradiction.

Rule 5 states that when a general proposition comes first, and is followed by particular instances, then the particular instances limit the scope of the general proposition. For example, '... you shall bring your offering of the cattle; of the herd and of the flock' (Leviticus 1.2). The word 'cattle' (*behemah*) is a general word, which might be construed as including undomesticated as well as domesticated animals. The particulars 'of the herd' and 'of the flock', however, should not be regarded as mere instances, but as limiting the term 'cattle' to these particulars, i.e. to domesticated animals, which alone may be offered as sacrifices.

Rule 6, on the other hand, states that if the particulars are given first, and then the general proposition, the opposite rule holds: the general term is not limited to the scope of the particulars. An example is, 'If a man delivereth to his neighbour an ass, or an ox, or a sheep, or any beast to keep, and it die ...' (Exodus 22.10). Here we have first the particulars, 'ass', 'ox', 'sheep', and then the general term, 'any beast'; and the rule demands that the general term must be regarded as including any animal whatsoever, not just those specified in the particulars. These two rules may, in fact, be regarded as a common-sense analysis of linguistic usage, in which the use of a general term, followed by particulars, is intended as a narrowing-down process, whereas the opposite procedure is intended as a widening process.

Rule 7 says that if a word has two meanings, the meaning that makes sense in the context should be adopted.

These very simple instances may serve to indicate the care with which the Pharisee sages read the Bible in their desire to amplify it and turn it into a comprehensive manual of law, in the light of usage, tradition, and ongoing legal practice. Some scholars have argued that the Pharisaic methods of biblical exegesis were derived from the Hellenistic world, being similar to those used by Alexandrian scholars in their exegesis of Homer, and in Hellenistic legal contexts. There may indeed have been some influence, but it would be a mistake to exaggerate its extent. Certain features of rabbinic logic are fundamentally different from Hellenistic logic. Thus the extensive use of the *a fortiori* argument in rabbinic logic has no real parallel in the Hellenistic literature, which does use the argument, but only in an inexact, rhetorical way, not as a formal argument with a developed theory. The basic formal argument in Hellenistic literature was the syllogism, as developed by Aristotle and his successors. An example of a syllogism is:

> all human beings are mortal;
> all women are human beings;
> therefore, all women are mortal.

The three classes concerned here are 'human beings', 'women' and 'mortals', and the syllogism shows relations of inclusion or exclusion between such classes. This suits the purposes of scientific classification, but not of law, which requires a logic of analogy, enabling us to decide which cases are similar to other cases, or dissimilar from them. This the Greeks never developed, and the achievement of the rabbis in developing a logic of analogy suitable for legal argument and the comparing of cases has not been sufficiently recognized.

The varied techniques of reasoning and argumentation developed in the Pharisee academies reflect an important feature of these academies—their atmosphere of constant discussion and debate. The Oral Torah was far from being a mere record of enactments and decisions; it was also a record of the disagreements and arguments leading up to each enactment. A student was expected to be familiar with all these arguments, including those that were outvoted. What the student was required to learn was not a list of laws, but rather the *process* by which laws were created. Thus when the Oral Torah eventually began to be put into written form in the Mishnah and other writings, it was the whole process of debate that was written down, with each separate authoritative rabbi being represented by the whole range of his opinions. We have, in effect, a large number of legal systems, each in the name of a different rabbi—the system of Rabbi Ishmael, the system of Rabbi Akiba, and so on, while it became the concern of the student to understand the internal coherence of each of these systems, even those that never became practical law. Why, the Mishnah asks, were all the rejected opinions recorded? One of the answers given is that thereby, if at any time a change in the law were required, there would be a wealth of precedents in the form of recorded dissenting opinions. This reply shows the fluidity of the process. But, even more importantly, it shows that in the Pharisee practice of Judaism, law was regarded not so much as something to be learnt, but as something to be created. The ideal was that the law was a continuous legislative process in which all Jews played an active role.

Clearly, to achieve mastery of this complex process of legislation unusual gifts were required, and this accounts for the emergence of the special class of sages or rabbis, trained in the academies (though this word is rather too formal for the training acquired by sitting at the feet of a master). But the process of law-making never became completely professionalized, because it was regarded as the concern of every Jew. The learning of the Oral Torah went on at many levels, and at every level some form of law-making, as well as law-learning, went on. Thus every adult Jew could function, at some time, as a judge in a civil case, for such cases were often tried by lay judges. The procedure was that if a person had a civil case against another person (say a case involving the repayment of a loan), a panel of three judges could be appointed consisting of one person nominated by one of the parties to the action, one judge nominated by the other party, and a third judge nominated by the other two judges. Such amateur courts were regarded as fully competent, but obviously the system would not work unless there was a high level of general education in the principles of the Oral Torah.

The morality of education

The ideal of the Pharisees, which was to some extent implemented in the Jewish society of the ancient world and the middle ages, was one of a literate, educated community, continually learning, and regarding the process of education as a religious duty. It was probably the most original contribution of the Pharisees to religion that they gave a religious dimension to the process of education, and imbued learning with an aura of morality.

The rabbinic work in which this ideal of education is especially embodied is *Abot*, one of the tractates of the Mishnah. This tractate became part of the liturgy, and can be found in *The Authorized Daily Prayer Book* as part of the Sabbath afternoon service. Its title means 'Fathers', and the tractate is commonly known in English as 'Ethics of the Fathers'. This title, however, is somewhat misleading, as the book is not about ethics in general, but about the ethics of education. It is a book about the teaching of morality, and the morality of teaching. It takes the form of a series of sayings recorded in the names of the chief teachers of the Pharisaic and rabbinic movements, from Simon the Just (of the third century B.C.E.) to Rabbi Joshua ben Levi (of the third century C.E.). This book contains the wisdom of the Pharisees and their successors, the rabbis, on such questions as, 'What makes a good pupil?', 'What makes a good teacher?', 'How does the learning process contribute to the building of character?' and many other such questions. Some samples will indicate the flavour of the book.

A group of sayings attributed to Hillel is the following.

> He used to say: a boor cannot be a fearer of sin; an ignorant man cannot be a saint; a bashful man cannot learn; and an impatient man cannot teach; nor can anyone who engages in much business become wise; and in a place where there are no men, strive to be a man.

> *(Abot 2.6)*

These sayings are not as miscellaneous as they look at first sight. They are all to do with the need for self-respect and a sense of human dignity as essential preconditions for the processes of learning and teaching. Hillel first stresses that virtue is not to be acquired by mere simplicity or innocence, but through striving by intellectual effort towards a higher standard. This is the theme of the whole book of *Abot*, which thus presents a view of mortality that contrasts with that of the New Testament, where virtue tends to be equated with innocence, and salvation is defined as the recovery of primal innocence (e.g. Matthew 18.3). A distinction is made in Hillel's saying between a 'boor' and an 'ignorant man'. A 'boor' is someone without cultivation or self-respect. He is defined as one who does not care about stains on his garments (Mishnah, Mikvaot 9.6). Such a person, who lacks a sense of his own dignity, is considered incapable even of ordinary morality. An 'ignorant man', on the other hand, can be a decent honourable person, but lacks the knowledge and insight that is necessary for sainthood. Only he who has intimate knowledge of the law can transcend it and attain to 'sainthood', which lies beyond the letter of the law. Hillel then goes on to say that 'a bashful man cannot learn', i.e. that self-confidence is necessary for the process of questioning one's teacher and putting forward objections and difficulties that makes an active learner; and, on the other hand, 'an impatient man cannot teach', for he does not feel sufficient respect for his pupils, and treats their questions with contempt. The next saying, 'nor can anyone who engages in much business become wise', is not just an exhortation to set aside sufficient time for study. It should be understood metaphorically, and means, 'Do not try to learn everything at once, but take your time, and learn each aspect thoroughly, one at a time'. For to be a 'know-all' is another way of showing lack of self-confidence; it is an inability to confess one's ignorance while one is slowly and gradually building up a stock of knowledge. Finally comes one of the great sayings of rabbinic literature, '... in a place where there are no men, strive to be a man'. This again is an injunction against over-humility, which might lead a person to question whether he is capable of sustaining a heroic role: if circumstances single you out to play such a role, play it.

In another series of sayings recorded in the name of Hillel, the theme is just the opposite, the need for humility in the learning process.

> Hillel says: Do not separate from the community; and do not trust yourself until the day of your death; and do not judge your neighbour until you come into his place; and do not say, 'A thing that it is impossible to understand!', because, in the end, it will be understood; and do not say, 'When I have leisure, I will study'—perhaps you will not have leisure.
>
> (*Abot* 2.5)

The saying, 'Do not separate from the community' might seem to conflict with the saying, 'in a place where there are no men, strive to be a man'. One saying stresses the need for community solidarity, whereas the other stresses the need to have the strength to stand out against the community and the herd-instinct. But there is no real conflict: one saying warns against over-confidence, and the other against over-humility. Where one knows that one is right and the majority wrong, stand up for the right; but do not withdraw from the community in the conviction of one's own superiority. This is a warning against the attitude of those such as the Qumran sect, and is an expression of the Pharisees' loyalty to the people as a whole. Further injunctions against pride are, 'do not trust yourself until the day of your death' and 'do not judge your neighbour until you come into his place'. This means that pride of learning should not make a person feel that he has overcome his own propensity to sin. Again, one should not imagine that something that is beyond one's own understanding is an insoluble problem; the process of learning is never-ending, and every person's understanding is limited. Finally comes an injunction to set aside regular times for study, for no mortal can plan ahead very confidently, and to postpone one's study may be to postpone it for ever. This ties in with another saying of Hillel's, 'If not now, when?'

Another passage, added later to the book in its liturgical use, outlines the qualities that are needed to attain the educational and moral benefits of the Torah.

> Greater is the Torah than priesthood or kingship; for kingship is acquired by thirty qualifications and the priesthood by twenty-four; but the Torah by forty-eight. And these are they: by study, by the hearing of the ear, by distinct pronunciation, by the discernment of the heart, by awe, by reverence, by humility, by cheerfulness; by attendance on the sages, by attaching oneself to colleagues, by discussion with disciples; by tranquillity, by knowledge of Scripture and Mishnah; by lessening one's business activities, by lessening sexual activity, by lessening self-indulgence, sleep, conversation and laughter; by patience, by a good heart, by loyalty to the wise, by acceptance of sufferings, by knowing one's place and rejoicing in one's portion, by making a fence to one's words, and by claiming no merit for oneself; by being beloved, loving God and loving one's fellow-creatures, loving just behaviour, loving rectitude, loving reproof; by shunning honour, by not feeling pride in one's learning, by not taking pleasure in making decisions; by bearing the yoke with one's fellow, by judging him charitably, by supporting him in the truth, and helping him in the achievement of peace; by adopting a settled manner of study; by asking questions; by answering questions; by listening and adding to what one hears; by learning in order to teach; and by learning in order to act; by making one's teacher wiser; by paying full attention to his teaching; and by saying a thing in the name of him who said it.
>
> (*Abot* 6.6)

Although this summary was written much later than our period, it is based largely on early sources and gives excellent expression to the Pharisee attitude towards education as bound up indissolubly with moral progress—an attitude that influenced all the subsequent history of Jews and Judaism down to the present day.

7

The Religious Year

All the Jewish sects of the first century built their religious life on the cycle of festivals outlined in the Bible. In the Gospels, too, we can see how Jesus' life was punctuated by these festivals, and by the other regularities and rites of Judaism, such as circumcision (Luke 2.21) and purification after childbirth (Luke 2.22). The chief festivals observed by all sects, in addition to the weekly celebration of the Sabbath, were the pilgrim festivals, Passover, Pentecost and Tabernacles, and the Days of Awe (nowadays often called the High Holy Days), the New Year and the Day of Atonement.

The pilgrim festivals (Hebrew, *regalim*) were so-called because it was commanded in the Bible that they could be celebrated in Jerusalem (Exodus 23.17, Deuteronomy 16.16). It was not expected, however, that all Jews would make the pilgrimage to Jerusalem three times every year, but only that they should do so as many times as they conveniently could during their lifetime; on most occasions, therefore, they celebrated these festivals at home. In fact, Jerusalem was always crowded during the festival times with pilgrims from all the far-flung places inhabited by Jews. A special pilgrim tithe (Deuteronomy 14.22–26) was set aside for consumption in Jerusalem on these festival occasions. This was called second tithe, and was payable four years in every six. In the other two years it was replaced by Poorman's Tithe (Deuteronomy 14.28–9 and 26.12). The pilgrim festivals were a powerful means by which Jews of the Diaspora retained their attachment to the Land of Israel. According to some scholars, the Psalms of Ascent (Psalms 120–34, each preceded by the words 'A Song of Ascents') were intended to be sung by pilgrims on their way to Jerusalem, but this explanation is not found in Jewish tradition.

The calendar

There was considerable disagreement between the various sects on the details of the calendar within which these festivals were set. The Jewish year was basically one of lunar months. Each new moon was celebrated as a minor festival, and each major festival was reckoned according to its position in a lunar calendar. It was necessary, however, to adjust this lunar calendar to the solar year; otherwise, the seasons would have got out of adjustment, and the spring festival of Passover, for example, would have slipped away into the winter. The different ways of carrying out this adjustment caused dissension between the sects. The Pharisees, whose calendar was accepted by the vast majority of the nation, adjusted it by adding a leap-month whenever this seemed necessary; when the condition of the ripening barley crop in early spring suggested that it would not be ripe in time for Passover, the month before Passover, Adar, would be repeated. In later rabbinic times, a fixed calendar was instituted, by which seven months were added during a cycle of nineteen years. The decision about when to insert a month, in earlier times including the first century, was made by the Sanhedrin, the supreme religious body, in which both Pharisees and Sadducees were represented. So it seems that Pharisees and Sadducees were agreed on the main outlines of the religious year, although they differed on certain details, especially on the date of Pentecost.

Other sects, however, disagreed much more radically with the Pharisee arrangements for the calendar. The Book of Jubilees, which was written in the second century B.C.E. advocates a calendar in which every year consists of exactly 364 days, and there are no leap years. Any sect that accepted this book as authoritative would not celebrate a single festival on the same day as the Pharisees; only the Sabbaths would coincide. The Qumran sect, whose writings, the Dead Sea Scrolls, were discovered in the present century, regarded the Book of Jubilees with reverence and followed its calendar.

This difference alone would be enough to ensure that the Qumran sect and the Pharisees regarded each other as heretical. But, in fact, there was a deeper difference between the two sects, even in this matter of the calendar, than a mere disagreement about dates. The difference was on the question, 'Who decides the calendar, God or man?' The Qumran sect, and any other sect that followed the Jubilees calendar (also found in 1 Enoch), thought of the whole year as immutably fixed by God. They claimed that their calendar was based on 'the laws of the Great Light of heaven', and they considered it an important feature of the perfection of their calendar that in it the festivals always began on the same day of the week. The Pharisees, on the other hand, had a much more relaxed attitude about this subject. They thought that God had handed over the regulation of the calendar to man, and that there was therefore no mystical, God-given date for each festival. Every festival could be postponed by decision of the Sanhedrin for commonsense reasons.

There is a story of the rabbis that illustrates this point. Towards the end of the first century, after the destruction of the Temple, when the Sanhedrin was situated at Jabneh (Jamnia) under the presidency of Rabban Gamaliel II, a disagreement arose between Rabbi Joshua and Rabban Gamaliel about the latter's determination of the beginning of the month of Tishri, during which the most awesome event of the Jewish religious year, the Day of Atonement, occurs. Gamaliel, a strict disciplinarian, then sent a message to Rabbi Joshua ordering the latter to appear before him on the day which on his (Rabbi Joshua's) reckoning was the Day of Atonement, 'carrying your staff and your money-purse'. Carrying a staff or money on the Day of Atonement was forbidden, and Rabban Gamaliel required a practical demonstration by Rabbi Joshua that he had relinquished his own ruling and accepted that of Rabban Gamaliel and his Court. Rabbi Joshua, in distress, consulted Rabbi Akiba, who counselled him to obey the command of Rabban Gamaliel, on the ground that God himself accepts the calendar rulings of duly appointed representatives of Israel even when they are wrong. This, argued Rabbi Akiba, can be proved from Scripture itself, which says, 'These are the set feasts of the Lord ... which you shall proclaim (Leviticus 23.4). This means, argued Rabbi Akiba; 'It is for you to proclaim them, says God. Whether they are at the right time or the wrong time, I have no other set feasts except the ones which are proclaimed on earth by the representatives of Israel.'

The story continues: 'On the day that was the Day of Atonement according to his own reckoning, Rabbi Joshua took his staff and his money-purse in his hand, and went to Jabneh to Rabban Gamaliel. Then Rabban Gamaliel stood up and kissed Rabbi Joshua on the head, and said to him, "Greetings to you, my master, and my disciple. You are my master in wisdom, but you are my disciple in that you have accepted my words"' (Mishnah, Rosh Hashanah 2.8–9).

Thus even in the matter of the calendar, the essential difference between the Pharisees and the smaller sects was the greater humanism of the Pharisees: their conviction that God respects the human intellect and makes allowances for its fallibility, preferring to accept fallible human decisions than to lay down inexorable rules for each detail of human life. The sectarians' abhorrence of the Pharisaic calendar was not matched by an equal abhorrence on the Pharisaic side: the Pharisees regarded the sectarians not as rebels against God, but as people who refused to accept decisions sanctioned by human authorities.

The pilgrim festivals

Despite this greater flexibility, the Pharisees were bound to the pattern of festivals laid down in the Bible, which indeed made a colourful religious year, each occasion having its own special flavour and atmosphere. The three pilgrim festivals, *Pesah*, or Passover, *Shavuot*, or Pentecost, and *Sukkot*, or Tabernacles, each had a seasonal aspect. Passover was the spring festival, marking the beginning of the corn harvest, with the offering in the Temple of the measure of barley-flour known as the *Omer* (see Leviticus 23.10–14 and Mishnah, Menahot 10.1–5). Pentecost (the word means in Greek, 'fiftieth', since it took place on the fiftieth day after Passover) took place at the end of the corn harvest, with the offering in the Temple of the Two Loaves (Leviticus 23.17), while Tabernacles was in the autumn, with the waving of palm-branches (Leviticus 23.40) and other ceremonies, to mark the ingathering of fruits and vines.

At the same time, each of these festivals was also given a historical aspect. Passover was regarded primarily as the anniversary of the Exodus from Egypt, and its main ceremony, the eating of the paschal lamb, commemorated this. Pentecost was seen as the anniversary of the giving of the Law on Mount Sinai. The Bible itself does not make this historical link, but treats Pentecost as a purely agricultural festival. The Pharisees, however, stressed the historical aspect and made it prominent in the festival liturgy. As for Tabernacles, the Bible does provide a somewhat tenuous historical link, by saying that the custom of dwelling in booths or tabernacles during this festival commemorated the years of wandering in the wilderness on the way to the Promised Land (Leviticus 23.43). Thus the festivals, while retaining their connection with the perennial cycle of nature, also took on a character of national celebration, marking the sacred history of the people of God.

Each of the pilgrim festivals receives some mention in the New Testament. Passover, of course, is the period of the story of the Passion. Jesus' entry into Jerusalem, the Last Supper, his trial and execution are all represented as taking place at Passover time. The Last Supper is generally thought of as a Passover meal, although in fact it does not present the features of one in the Gospel accounts—for example, there is no mention of unleavened bread, the eating of bitter herbs or any of the other distinctive features of a Passover meal. Some scholars have argued that Jesus' entry into Jerusalem actually took place at the time of the autumn festival of Tabernacles, not at Passover, in the spring. Some of the details recorded in the Gospels support this view: for example, Jesus was greeted by the waving of palm branches (John 12.13), which were used in the ceremonies of Tabernacles, not of Passover, when they were not available in Jerusalem. Moreover, the cry of the crowd, 'Hosanna', was typical of the Tabernacles ceremonies, not of Passover. Further, the incident in which Jesus cursed the fig tree for not bearing fruit is hard to understand if this took place in the spring, when fig trees could not be expected to bear fruit, but quite understandable in the autumn (Matthew 21.19). The strange description in the Gospel of John of a visit to Jerusalem by Jesus at the time of the festival of Tabernacles (John 7) has no parallel in the other Gospels. It may well be that this visit, represented as only a preliminary one, was in fact identical with the Triumphal Entry. If Jesus was in fact arrested in the autumn and executed by the Romans in the spring, this would give adequate time for the whole train of events, which are implausibly crowded into a single week in the Gospel accounts.

The festival of Pentecost receives prominent mention in the book of Acts, for it was on this date that the apostles were 'filled with the Holy Spirit'. This experience is often regarded as the foundation day of the Christian Church, and the miraculous events with which it is surrounded by the author of Acts show that he regarded it as having great historical significance. It seems likely, as many scholars have suggested, that the Jewish significance of Pentecost, as the anniversary of the giving of the Torah on Mount Sinai, is relevant here. It seemed right that the new religion, Christianity, should begin on the anniversary of the founding of Judaism. This, however, may be an interpretation after the event by the author of Acts, for the leaders of the so-called 'Jerusalem Church' probably did not regard themselves as founders of a new religion, but as loyal adherents of Judaism.

The Days of Awe

Even more important than the pilgrim festivals were the solemn High Holy Days, the New Year and the Day of Atonement, in which the key theme was repentance. The New Year festival is actually not referred to as such in the Bible, which simply says that the first day of the seventh month, Tishri, is to be celebrated as 'a holy convocation'. The only New Year day recognised in the Bible explicitly is the first of Nisan, shortly before Passover, in the spring (Exodus 12.2), although no special religious celebration is ordained for this day (apart from the usual observance of new moon). The month of Nisan is treated thoughout the Bible as the first month. So why was the first of the seventh month, Tishri, regarded as the New Year festival, and, as such, a day of solemn rededication and repentance? The answer seems to be that the year beginning with Nisan was derived, together with all the names of the months, from Babylonian practice; whereas the year beginning in the autumn derives from Canaanite practice, and is bound up with agriculture, in which a new beginning is made after the period of autumn harvesting. Some of the older Canaanite names for the months are preserved in the Bible (Abib, for Nisan, for example), and there is an indirect reference to the old agricultural calendar in Exodus 23.16, which refers to 'the feast of ingathering at the end of the year' (see also Exodus 34.22). It seems then that the idea that the autumn is the beginning of the calendar is older than the Bible, and survived the Bible's attempt to substitute the Babylonian calendar. This is a good example of how the 'traditions', of which the Pharisees were the acknowledged custodians, might sometimes be of such great antiquity that they pre-dated the canonization of the Bible.

The strange result was that there were two New Years in the calendar, one invested with great religious awe, but actually situated at the start of the seventh month, and the other, having no special aura about it, yet firmly placed at the beginning of the recognized calendar. From a religious point of view, the autumn New Year, known as *Rosh Hashanah*, was the day when one reviewed one's deeds of the past year and dedicated oneself anew for the coming year.

Indeed, the whole series of autumn festivals formed a single dramatic unit, moving from repentance to rejoicing. The New Year, on the first of Tishri, was followed by the Day of Atonement on the tenth of Tishri, and between these two dates were the Days of Penitence, in which rites of self-examination were intensified. New Year itself was a festival, in which feasting and enjoyment of a moderate kind were encouraged, but the Day of Atonement was a solemn fast-day, spent in prayer and supplication for mercy before the throne of God in his aspect of Judge. Then, on the fifteenth of Tishri, began the festival of Tabernacles, the most joyful festival of the whole year.

During the first 70 years of the first century, the Temple was still standing, so all the festivals described so far were accompanied by special sacrifices there, performed by the priests in accordance with the prescriptions laid down in the Bible. On the New Year and the Day of Atonement, the rites in the Temple were especially elaborate. A special rite of the New Year was the blowing of the *shofar*, an instrument made from an animal's horn. This ceremonious sounding of an alarm was understood as a serious call to every person's conscience, so that he would busy himself with deeds of repentance, such as giving reparation for any wrongs committed, and placating anyone whom he had needlessly offended. A special rite of the Day of Atonement was the sacrifice of the scapegoat (Leviticus 16.10), which bore the sins of the people into the desert. Also on this day, the High Priest entered the Holy of Holies, which could not be entered at any other time, to make atonement for Israel (Leviticus 16.15–17). On the Day of Atonement the High Priest announced absolution to the people in the words of Scripture ('For on this day shall atonement be made for you to cleanse you; from all your sins shall ye be clean before the Lord' (Leviticus 16.30)) using in public for the only time in the year the Name of God in its explicit form, i.e. the fully vocalized Tetragrammaton (the name of four letters), which was usually pronounced only in a disguised form.

Animal sacrifices

Some explanation is necessary, at this point, of the practice of animal sacrifice in the Temple, as a means of expiation. It should not be thought that the sacrifices were held to have some magical efficacy in wiping away sins. On the contrary, they were regarded as having no efficacy at all, in the absence of genuine repentance and reparation. This, at any rate, was the view of the Pharisees. There was nothing new about this attitude towards animal sacrifices, of course. It is found in the biblical prophets (e.g. Isaiah 1.11–17, Jeremiah 6.19–20, Amos 5.21–24) and in the intertestamental literature (e.g. Ecclesiasticus 7.9, 31.21–31, 32.14–26). It is expressed in the Mishnah as follows.

He who says, 'I will sin, and repent: I will sin and repent'; he will never achieve repentance. 'I will sin, and the Day of Atonement will atone'; the Day of Atonement does not atone. Transgressions between man and God—the Day of Atonement atones. Transgressions between man and his neighbour—the Day of Atonement does not atone, until he appeases his neighbour.

(Mishnah, Yoma 8.9)

This passage warns against a mechanical attitude towards atonement, as if it can be achieved by some form of words or some empty rite, without a genuine change of the heart. A person who says that he repents, but secretly reserves his intention to commit the same sinful act again, has not truly repented. Similarly, a person who sins with the thought that his sin will be wiped away by the rites of the Day of Atonement is deluding himself, for the Day of Atonement has no effect on such a sin. Again, a person who sins against his neighbour and repents, but fails to make reparation for the harm he has done, cannot expect the Day of Atonement to make up for this deficit. Only sins against God (e.g. transgressions of the Sabbath), where repentance alone is sufficient, can be finally wiped away by the Day of Atonement.

It should be noted that the above remarks apply not just to the sacrifices of the Day of Atonement, but to the whole Jewish sacrificial system. Sin-offerings were brought not to effect a primary atonement for the sin, but only as the final step in a process of atonement. The commonest form of sin-offering was brought when a person discovered that he had committed a transgression unwittingly. In such a case, repentance was not required, except to the extent that negligence was involved; but the dismay caused by the realization that one had unwittingly performed a forbidden act, and the resultant sense of distance from God, were repaired by the bringing of the sacrifice (see Leviticus 4 and 5.1–19). On the other hand, if a sin was committed intentionally, only repentance and reparation could atone for it (Leviticus 5.20–26), and the sacrifice that was brought after this process had been completed was not, in itself, an atonement, but only a last step in the process, giving a sense of finality and peace to the repentant person.

Many sacrifices offered in the Temple, however, had nothing to do with sin, but were offered in gratitude to God. Such offerings (known as 'peace offerings' and 'thank offerings') had the character of a meal shared with God, for the offerer ate part of the sacrificed animal. Moreover, by no means all the offerings were animal sacrifices; a great many were vegetable offerings, in the form of meal offerings and libations of wine.

Thus the whole Jewish sacrificial system had moved in the direction of seeing sacrifices as gifts to God, rather than as vicarious sufferers for the sacrificer's sins. This being so, it was no great shock to the Jewish religious scheme of atonement when the Temple was destroyed and all sacrifices ceased. Sorrow was felt that the final link in the chain of atonement had been removed, but it was also felt that the essential links still remained, for repentance and reparation could be achieved without the Temple. Many sayings of the rabbis assert that prayer, study and the performance of loving deeds take the place of the sacrifices in the post-Temple world as the clinching factor in atonement; and this does not reflect any change of viewpoint, for even before the destruction of the Temple, the sacrifices were not given a primary role. While the Temple stood, the biblical injunctions to perform sacrifices were in force, but since God himself had removed the Temple, this obligation had also been removed. Hence no blame or deficiency in atonement could be attributed to any person, who, through circumstances beyond his control, was not able to offer the biblical sacrifices.

It must be added, however, that there was some tension or conflict between the Pharisee attitude towards expiation and the dramatic rituals of the Day of Atonement, especially that of the scapegoat. The Bible describes this ritual as follows:

> And Aaron shall lay both his hands upon the head of the live goat, and confess over him all the iniquities of the children of Israel, and all their transgressions in all their sins, putting them upon the head of the goat, and shall send him away by the hand of a fit man into the wilderness. And the goat shall bear upon him all their iniquities unto a land not inhabited: and he shall let go the goat in the wilderness.
>
> (Leviticus 16.21–22)

In Pharisee teaching, this ceremony was symbolic only, and the goat did not in any real sense bear the iniquities of the people, which had to be expiated by repentance. Here the Pharisees were simply continuing the attitude of the biblical prophets, who inveighed against a wrong, magical theory of the sacrifices. For example, the prophet Micah wrote:

> Will the Lord be pleased with thousands of rams, or with ten thousands of rivers of oil? shall I give my firstborn for my transgression, the fruit of my body for the sin of my soul? He hath shewed thee, O man, what is good; and what doth the Lord require of thee, but to do justly, and to love mercy, and to walk humbly with thy God?
>
> (Micah 6.7–8)

There is no evidence that the prophets wished to abolish the sacrifices, but they wished them to be understood as symbols of repentance, not as substitutes for it. To kill an animal as a vicarious victim to carry away one's sins, the prophet Michah is saying, is no better than to carry out a human sacrifice for the same purpose.

Yet the common people, watching the impressive ceremony of the scapegoat, must have felt that the animal was indeed carrying away their sins. It is this common, primitive feeling, not the rationalism of the Pharisees, or the injunctions of the prophets, that prompted the view of Jewish sacrifice found in the New Testament, where the death of Jesus, interpreted as a sacrifice carrying away the sins of the world, is likened to the animal sacrifices of the Temple. Thus Paul likened the death of Jesus to the sacrifice of the paschal lamb (1 Corinthians 5.7), so reverting to the oldest and most primitive stratum of Israelite religion, in which the paschal lamb was regarded as a blood-victim warding off evil, rather than as a joyful meal of gratitude to God for the deliverance of the Exodus. The most thorough-going statement of this analogy between the death of Jesus and the older Israelite theory of animal sacrifice is in the Epistle to the Hebrews, chapter 9, culminating in the sentence, 'And almost all things are by the law purged with blood; and without shedding of blood is no remission' (Hebrews 9.22).

The Sabbath and the minor festivals

Important as all the above-described festivals were, the weekly celebration of the Sabbath was regarded as more important than all of them (with the single exception of the Day of Atonement, the holiest occasion of the year). The Sabbath was regarded by the Pharisees as an occasion of joy, and as a foretaste of the World to Come, which is called in the rabbinic literature, 'the day that is all Sabbath'. In addition to the Sabbath services in the synagogue, including the readings from the Bible and the sermon, there were observances in the home, which were developed by the Pharisees. These included the lighting of the Sabbath lights by the mistress of the home to welcome in the Sabbath, a ceremony alluded to by Roman authors, including Juvenal, and the reciting of the *Kiddush* ('Sanctification') by the master of the home. The Kiddush was recited over a cup of wine, and its two blessings were for the gift of wine and for God's sanctifying of the Sabbath. The Sabbath was a day of rest and enjoyment, on which the mind was to be detached from week-day worries. It was considered meritorious to honour the Sabbath by wearing one's best clothes and having the best of food; and an atmosphere of comfort, tranquillity and enjoyment was to be cultivated.

All the religious occasions of the calendar described so far are derived from biblical injunctions, the observance of the Sabbath being included in the Ten Commandments themselves. But some other occasions were observed that were regarded as of lesser importance, being instituted by man, not by God. One of these was the minor festival of *Purim*, which although contained in the Bible, was not a Divine ordinance of the Torah but, as the Book of Esther makes clear, a humanly ordained institution (Esther 9.20–21). This was a festival of merry-making, at which the drinking of wine was encouraged, and a spirit of revelry prevailed. The Book of Esther was read in the synagogue, commemorating the deliverance that gave rise to the festival. Another minor festival of deliverance was *Hanukkah* ('Dedication'), commemorating the rededication of the Temple after the victory of Judas Maccabaeus over the Seleucid Greeks (1 Maccabees 4.59). This was a more sober festival, celebrating the religious, rather than the national, aspects of the deliverance, chiefly by the lighting of the Hanukkah lamps. This festival is mentioned in the New Testament (John 10.22). During the first century, other events in the story of the Maccabees were also celebrated, as we learn from a book called Megillat Ta'anit, the earliest surviving writing of the Pharisees. In the second century, however, these days were abolished from the calendar, and only the celebration of Hanukkah remained—a good example of the constitutional power of the rabbis to reverse, if it was felt necessary, decisions of previous rabbinic councils.

A more gloomy occasion was the fast-day of the Ninth of Ab, held in commemoration of the destruction of the First Temple by Nebuchadnezzar, and also, after 70 C.E., in commemoration of the destruction of the Second Temple. This was a day of mourning and repentance. Other fast-days could be proclaimed by the Sanhedrin when occasion called for special supplication, especially when there was a protracted drought.

So the Judaism of the first century celebrated in its religious calendar both the cycle of the seasons and the events of sacred history, and, in addition, the solemn season of the High Festivals provided the occasion for searching the conscience, and for self-renewal for the coming year.

8

Ritual Purity

Many misconceptions can be found, even in the writings of scholars, on the topic of ritual purity. These misconceptions have led to some very mistaken theories about the Pharisees, and also to some mistaken would-be solutions to problems in New Testament scholarship, such as, 'Why did the Pharisees disapprove of tax-gatherers?'

Ritual purity must, first of all, be defined. It has nothing to do with the dietary laws, by which certain foods were forbidden to Jews as 'unclean'. Ritual purity laws are of an entirely different kind, and may be found in the Bible in Leviticus 11.24–40, 13, 15, and Numbers 19.14–22. These laws state that certain substances are regarded as defiling, so that if a person comes in contact with these substances, he must not enter the holy area of the Temple, or eat any holy food, unless he has first undergone a procedure of purification. (The case of the leper, who becomes unclean through a defiling disease, rather than from being in contact with a defiling substance, is a special one.) Some substances were more defiling than others: contact with a human corpse defiled a person for seven days, whereas contact with human semen defiled only for one day.

Impurity and sinfulness

It was not regarded as sinful to become ritually unclean. On the contrary, it was regarded as inevitable that a person, in the course of ordinary living, would become ritually unclean in one way or another. Indeed, a person might well become unclean through some meritorious activity that had the full blessing of the Torah. Thus it was a religious duty to take part in a funeral, but this participation meant being under one roof with the corpse, which produced ritual uncleanness (Numbers 19.14). Only the priests were forbidden to take part in funerals (except of near relatives) on grounds of avoiding corpse-uncleanness, and even they were permitted to become unclean from other sources. For example, priests, like other Jews, were under a religious obligation to have intercourse with their wives (Exodus 21.10), and yet sexual intercourse was one of the causes of ritual impurity (Leviticus 15.16–18). Even in the case of corpse-uncleanness, a priest was not only permitted, but obliged, to incur it in certain emergency circumstances, such as if he came across an unburied corpse, and there was no-one else at hand to bury it.

Thus there was no sin, and there might even be merit, in becoming ritually unclean. Where sinfulness did enter the picture was that it was regarded as wrong to defile holy areas or foodstuffs; so a person who, knowing himself to be in a state of ritual uncleanness, deliberately entered a holy area or touched or ate a holy meal, thereby committed a sin, for which he required repentance and atonement. Even this, however, was subject to exceptions, for, as we have seen in the case of David and the shewbread (see chapter 3), even the sanctities of the Holy of Holies were set aside in a case of danger to human life.

Thus ritual impurity was regarded much as we regard physical uncleanness, or dirtiness. It would be impossible to make a rule that people are to avoid ever getting dirty, for not only would this be impracticable, but many of the most essential activities of life, including agriculture, coal-mining and engineering, not to mention activities such as heart surgery or mountain climbing or oil painting, involve getting dirty. But one can and does make a rule that dirt should be removed, however heroically or necessarily acquired, before, say, sitting down at the dinner table, or attending a party. This is a matter of courtesy, and it would be regarded as an insult to one's hosts to flout this rule. In ancient Palestine, it was thought (on the basis of inspired biblical texts) that there were certain invisible kinds of dirt that had to be removed before one could enter God's house, or eat at his table, even though ordinary life, and also many admirable activities, made the acquisition of this kind of dirt inevitable. Bathing in a pool was all that was necessary to remove this 'dirt', and then one could enter the Temple without discourtesy to God. The conception of this invisible kind of dirt was not dissimilar to our modern conception of invisible contamination by germs or bacteria, which again requires procedures of purification without implying any moral criticism of the persons being purified.

It follows from the above picture that ordinary people did not have much need to worry about ritual purity most of the time. It was only when they wanted to enter the Temple precincts, which was usually at festival times, that they had to take care to be in a state of ritual purity. Their food did not count as holy food, so they did not have to worry about contaminating it, and could eat it in a state of uncleanness, in accordance with the biblical verse, 'The clean and the unclean shall eat of them alike' (Deuteronomy 12.22). The priests, on the other hand, did have a much greater concern with ritual purity. They served in the Temple, and had to be ritually clean during this service, which however was limited in extent, since the priests were divided into 'courses' and shifts. More important, they ate the priestly food throughout the year, and this counted as holy food which had to be protected from contamination. On the other hand, the priests were not obliged to eat the priestly food, and many might prefer on occasion to eat ordinary food, which did not require them to undergo purification. So even priests might be in a state of ritual uncleanness for much of the time without incurring any sin, provided only that they avoided corpse-contamination, which was specifically forbidden to them at all times (though, of course, if they incurred it inadvertently this was not reckoned a sin).

The *haberim*

In addition, however, to the ordinary people and the priests, there was a third group that must be considered in relation to the topic of ritual purity. This was the group known as the *haberim*, or 'table-fellowships'. These were laymen (i.e. non-priests) who formed an association (*haburah*) for the purpose of practising ritual purity. The purpose of these associations has been subject to much misunderstanding.

The *haberim* (literally, 'companions' or 'fellows'), being non-priests, were not obliged to be in a state of ritual purity while eating their food, but they undertook voluntarily to 'eat their food in purity'. In practice, this meant that they immersed themselves in the ritual pool (*miqvah*) before their meals, even though these meals consisted of ordinary food (*hullin*), not priestly food (*terumah*) which, as laymen, they were not entitled to eat. The whole exercise was a kind of imitation by laymen of the practice of the priests, in which ordinary food was treated as if it were holy food. In fact, however, the *haberim* did not attempt to attain quite the same standard of ritual purity as the priests, since their aim was merely not to impart impurity to ordinary food. Because ordinary food was regarded as not so susceptible to uncleanness as holy food, the aim of *haberim* could be attained without reaching the highest degree of ritual cleanness, and they were satisfied therefore with attaining the second degree of cleanness.

The main point to understand about the *haberim* is that they were doing something voluntary. They formed small associations or societies for the purpose of practising a non-obligatory exercise of piety, but this does not mean that they regarded ordinary people, who did not undertake this unusual life, as being sinners or beyond the pale, any more than Catholic monks or friars regard people who live ordinary lives as being wicked. It has always been a feature of Jewish religious life that some people will form small fellowships in order to pursue a religious aim beyond the call of ordinary duty. In the case of the *haberim* there was also a practical aim, in addition to personal piety. There is evidence in the rabbinic writings that members of the ritual purity associations were called upon to handle the separation of the priestly tithes (*terumah*) from the crops. Once separated, these tithes became holy, and care had to be taken not to commit sacrilege by imparting impurity to them. Hence, when the time came, the farmer would send for a member of the local purity fellowship, who would remove the required quantity of produce and put it into earthenware jars, ready for collection by the priests. It was therefore very useful to have a class of people who took care to keep themselves in a state of unusual cleanness, and could be called on to handle holy substances at the times when the farmers were ready to separate the tithes, so that the *terumah* was never touched by anyone in a state of ritual uncleanness.

From the standpoint of personal piety, however, the aim of the *haberim* was to bridge the gap between the priests and the laity by providing a way of life in which some laymen could voluntarily live something like the priestly life. Behind this aim lay well-known concepts of Judaism: that all Jews were priests, since the nation was called in Scripture, 'a kingdom of priests and a holy nation' (Exodus 19.6), and also that the whole land Israel, being a holy land, deserved to have its produce treated as holy food, even when not consecrated to the use of the Temple. These concepts, however, were never carried to the point of abolishing the distinction between priests and laymen, for this distinction had Scriptural authority. There was, after all, a great difference between the practice of the *haberim* and the practice of the priests whom they were imitating, for if a *haber* failed to eat his food in purity, he was only breaking his voluntary undertaking, whereas a priest who failed to eat his holy food in purity was guilty of a serious sacrilege.

The result of all this was that the *haberim* formed a numerically small group that never aimed at converting the whole Jewish people to their way of life, but regarded themselves as pursuing one of the options offered by Jewish piety. It should be remembered that another option open to a pious person was to join a burial society, which concerned itself with laying out the dead and arranging their burial. This was never regarded as a matter for a professional undertaker and, even today, Jewish burial societies exist, known as *hevra qadisha*, for this purpose. Members of such a society were dedicating themselves to a life of ritual impurity, for contact with a corpse was one of the prime causes of impurity. Yet members of a burial society were regarded as living a religious, dedicated life just as much as members of a *haburah*, whose aim was to attain a high degree of ritual purity. Each of the many forms of pious society had its individual aim and service to the community at large, and none of them regarded non-members as sinners.

It seems that most of the *haberim* came from the Pharisees, although we do find mention of them among the Sadducees and Samaritans too. This does not mean, however, that all Pharisees were *haberim*, or that the Pharisee movement should be altogether defined in terms of the aims of the 'table-fellowships'. This is a mistake made by certain nineteenth-century scholars, which has unfortunately been revived more recently. The Pharisee movement as a whole had much wider aims than merely to pursue one pious concept. As we have seen, the Pharisees were the guardians of the whole Oral Torah, and their aims covered the entire spiritual horizon of biblical prophetic Judaism.

One cause of the mistake of identifying the Pharisees entirely with the 'table-fellowships' is purely linguistic. It happens that the Hebrew word for 'Pharisees' (*perushim*) also has several other meanings, one of which is indeed 'members of a ritual purity fellowship'. The basic meaning of the word *perushim* is 'separate people', and it can apply to any body of people set apart by having some common programme different from that of others. Sometimes the word, as found in the rabbinic literature, has a pejorative use, meaning 'sectarians' or 'heretics'. For example, the *birkat ha-minim*, or 'blessing against heretics', one of the Eighteen Blessings that form the central prayer of the Jewish liturgy, is found in an early version with the word *perushim* instead of *minim* in the sense of 'heretics'. As explained earlier (chapter 1), the Pharisees probably received their name originally as a term of reproach, which later became a name of honour. Unfortunately, it is not easy to distinguish *perushim* meaning 'Pharisees' from *perushim* in other meanings. One has to decide its meaning from the context, and this has led to mistakes, particularly in relation to one important passage in the Mishnah (Hagigah 2.7), where many scholars translate *perushim* wrongly as 'Pharisees', where the correct translation is 'members of a ritual purity society'.

New Testament interpretation

We may now turn to certain theories in New Testament interpretation which can be seen to be seriously mistaken in the light of the above discussion.

Eating with tax gatherers

Why did the Pharisees disapprove of Jesus' consorting with tax collectors (see Matthew 9.10–13, Mark 2.14–17, Luke 5.27–32)? The explanation often offered is is that the Pharisees were concerned here with the question of ritual purity. Pharisees themselves, it is argued, would not consort with tax collectors because these men were regarded as especially ritually unclean; to prove this, a passage in the Mishnah is cited: 'If tax gatherers entered a house all that is within it becomes unclean' (Mishnah, Tohorot 7.6).

However, if Jesus was not a member of one of the voluntary ritual-purity societies, there would be no objection to his eating together with people who were in a state of ritual uncleanness, since this was specifically permitted by the Bible. There was nothing sinful in being ritually unclean, and neither tax gatherers nor any other Jews would be censured on this score as 'sinners', unless of course they entered the Temple or ate holy food while in this condition.

Moreover, tax gatherers were not regarded as more ritually unclean than other people. When the Mishnah says, 'If tax gatherers entered a house all that is within it becomes unclean', it is simply pointing to the fact that tax gatherers, when they entered a house for the purpose of assessing its owner for tax, were in the habit of handling everything in the house to assess its worth. The house referred to in this context is that of a *haber*, who was observing a special regime of ritual purity. If he came home and found that his house had been broken into in his absence, he had to judge how far the contents of the house had been interfered with and so rendered ritually unclean. If the intruder were merely a burglar (the Mishnah tells us in the sequel) he can assume that only those places where the burglar's tracks appeared had been rendered unclean. If he had reason to believe, however, that the intruder was a tax gatherer, he had to assume that everything had been rendered unclean. This is not because a tax gatherer is more unclean than a burglar or any other person—only more meddlesome. If, on the other hand, the owner of the house was not a *haber*, he had no need to worry about any uncleanness caused to his belongings, since these would be in a state of ritual uncleanness all the time; with perfect justification, because he had made no undertaking to avoid ritual uncleanness in circumstances where the law did not demand this.

This example shows how easy it is to get hold of the wrong end of the stick in ritual-purity matters, and come to all kinds of wrong conclusions. If we turn back to the actual Gospel texts, we note that nothing is said in them about ritual purity in connection with tax gatherers. The complaint made against Jesus by the Pharisees is, 'Why eateth your Master with publicans and sinners?' to which Jesus replies, 'They that be whole need not a physician, but they that are sick'. The point is that the 'publicans', or tax gatherers, were sinners. This does not mean that there was nothing much wrong with them, and that they were merely seedy, disreputable people whom the Pharisees disdained for social or hygienic reasons. In reality they were villainous people, whose conduct was that of gangsters. We know about their behaviour from other sources: they were violent and rapacious. They drove many people to suicide or outlawry, and were notorious for their use of torture. The infamous tax-farming system meant that the only limit to the exaction of taxes was the ability of the tax farmer, who had bought the right to tax from the Roman government, to extort money from his unfortunate victims. The tax farmers hired the worst elements of the local population to help them in their work of extortion, so these minor tax officials were regarded as criminals and traitors, who had lost all loyalty to their own people.

Thus when Jesus consorted with tax gatherers, he was consorting with real sinners, not merely with people who failed to conform to some standard of etiquette. Jesus ate with them not for the pleasure of their company but because he hoped to bring them to repentance, and this meant that he hoped to persuade them to give up their criminal way of life. Thus we see that Zacchaeus (Luke 19.2–10), a tax gatherer whom Jesus brought to repentance, vowed to give up his way of life and to restore his ill-gotten gains to his victims. Some Pharisees may have criticized Jesus for consorting with tax gatherers and other sinners on the ground that his hopes were too naïve. Someone who associates with gangsters, they may have thought, is more likely to become corrupted by such companions than to bring them to repentance. This view was perfectly sensible in ordinary circumstances, but what buoyed up Jesus' hopes was his conviction that the kingdom of God was at hand. He was engaged in a great campaign of repentance, directed towards the 'lost sheep of the house of Israel', and, like other Jewish Messiah-figures of whom we have record, he thought that the more Jews could be induced to repent, the more the coming of the kingdom would be confirmed. Thus he explained that it was more urgent to approach sinners than to enjoy the company of the pious. There is no need to suppose that he was being sarcastic when he said that the Pharisees were 'those that be whole'.

This is not to say that Jesus was unusual in his emphasis on repentance. The Pharisees, in their sermons and writings and prayers, continually emphasize that God is merciful to the repentant sinner, who is more beloved to God than he who has never sinned. There is a difference, however, between this general attitude and Jesus' urgent messianic campaign, which broke through normal commonsense considerations. On the other hand it is wrong to say, as some scholars have argued, that the Pharisees did not believe that tax gatherers could ever be accepted as penitents. The Tosefta discusses the penitent tax gatherer with sympathy, pointing out that his case is especially difficult because he has robbed so many victims that he does not know even who they are; consequently, restitution, which is essential for full repentance, is difficult for him. The advice of the Tosefta is that he should give money to public works or charity, if he cannot return it to his victims personally, and this will be accepted by God as restitution (Tosefta, Baba Metzia 8.16). Exactly the same policy was adopted by Zacchaeus, who promised to repay his known victims and also to give half of his goods to the poor (Luke 9.8). Thus Jesus' policy towards tax gatherers, although coloured by his unusual messianic expectations, was perfectly in accord with Pharisee thinking.

The Good Samaritan

Another important instance where much New Testament scholarship has been misled through wrong ideas about ritual purity is in the interpretation of the parable of the Good Samaritan (Luke 10.30–37). In this parable, a man is wounded and stripped by robbers. A priest and Levite, seeing him lying wounded, fail to help him, and 'pass by on the other side'. A Samaritan, on the other hand, has pity on him, binds his wounds and brings him to an inn, where he arranges nursing for him.

An explanation often given for this story is that the priest and the Levite were motivated by concern for ritual purity. The wounded man might die, and then the priest or the Levite, if they were tending him, might incur corpse-uncleanness. Some commentators, offering this explanation, seem to feel that they are thereby *excusing* the priest and the Levite, who were allegedly motivated by religious considerations, not by mere selfishness and unconcern. Jesus, however, it is argued, by telling this parable, taught the new lesson that helping one's fellow man is more important than ritual purity.

However, the story does not make the slightest mention of ritual purity. Even a cursory study of the rabbinic sources will show that ritual purity was regarded as unimportant compared with the saving of human life. A priest who neglected to save human life because he wanted to preserve his ritual cleanness would have been regarded as either a madman or a criminal. As for Levites (subordinate priests not descended from Aaron, but of the tribe of Levi), they were not even commanded to avoid ritual impurity from corpses, so the whole question does not even arise in their case. A full priest was commanded not to incur corpse-uncleanness, but this command was overridden by any emergency involving danger to human life. Moreover, this command was even overridden by the obligation to bury a corpse found abandoned at the wayside (*met mitzvah*). Even a High Priest was obliged to lay aside his priestly dignity and bury such a corpse. So this explanation of the Good Samaritan parable is riddled with mistakes.

The belief that this explanation excuses the priest and the Levite, while demonstrating the superior moral stance of Jesus, results from ignorance of first-century Judaism. Jesus' stance was exactly the same as that of the other Jews of his period. The point of Jesus' parable is simply that rank does not ensure right conduct. The priest and the Levite, who should have known better, failed in their moral duty, whereas the lowly Samaritan fulfilled the Torah by showing compassion. The moral of this parable is one that was a commonplace in the Pharisee sermons of the time, where there was no tendency to regard priests and Levites as above criticism.

Eating with unwashed hands

There is a tendency among certain scholars to read into the text of the New Testament references to ritual purity when they are not relevant to the true understanding of the text. One passage always held to be concerned with ritual purity is the following:

> And when they saw some of the disciples eat bread with defiled, that is to say, with unwashen, hands, they found fault. For the Pharisees, and all the Jews, except they wash their hands oft, eat not, holding the tradition of the elders. And when they come from the market, except they wash, they eat not. And many other things there be which they have received to hold, as the washing of cups, and pots, brasen vessels, and of tables.
>
> (Mark 7.2–4; see also Matthew 15.1–11)

This passage may indeed be referring to ritual purity, but this is by no means certain. The evidence from the rabbinic writings is that the washing of hands for ritual purity purposes, so far from being 'a tradition of the elders' in the time of Jesus, was a late institution, first enacted at about 65 C.E. Earlier, the only form of ritual washing was of the whole body. The passage may well be referring not to ritual-purity washing, but to plain hygienic washing of hands, which was indeed an ancient practice, not only among the Jews but among all civilised peoples. As for the 'washing of cups, and pots, brasen vessels, and of tables', this might be done by *haberim* for ritual purity purposes, but certainly not by 'all Jews', who would however wash their utensils for other religious purposes; notably before Passover, to clear away possible traces of leaven before the 'feast of unleavened bread' (this pre-Passover washing of utensils is performed by Jews even today), or when changing the use of vessels from meat meals to milk meals, because meat and milk are forbidden together.

Jesus' argument, when challenged on the question of washing of hands, reinforces the view that we have here a matter of hygiene, not ritual purity. His argument (Mark 7.14–23) is physical: that which enters a man from outside cannot defile him, because it is purged by the bodily processes of digestion and defecation. This is an argument against the possibility of physical contamination, not ritual contamination, which was never regarded as having any physical effects on the body.

It seems that the argument between the Pharisees and Jesus turns on the question of whether hygienic precautions are necessary for someone dedicated to a life of holiness. We know from the rabbinic writings that a certain section of the Pharisees known as the Hasidim ('saints') (see chapter 2), did not approve of hygienic precautions, regarding them as showing lack of faith in God, who would not allow a person who was free from sin to fall into disease. It has often been remarked that Jesus shows many of the traits of the Hasidim (notably his miracle cures and his injunction to 'take no thought for the morrow'), and he may well have been a Pharisee of this type. The main body of the Pharisees, although admiring the Hasidim for their saintliness, took the commonsense view that ordinary people needed to have regard for hygiene, and were culpably careless of human life if they neglected such precautions. Arguments took place between the two wings of the Pharisee movement on this question, and Jesus' argument on the question of the washing of hands was thus an intra-Pharisee argument, not a confrontation between widely opposed antagonists. Jesus is saying that God provides, in the natural constitution of the body, sufficient protection against any harmful substances that may be taken into the body through the mouth; whereas the Pharisees argue that unwashed hands may cause disease, and are therefore forbidden as infringing the religious duty to guard the health of the body.

Incidentally, the idea that when Jesus said, 'There is nothing from without a man, that entering into him can defile him' (Mark 7.15) he meant to abolish the Jewish dietary laws, is a later Church interpretation. It is clear from the practice of the early Jerusalem Church that they had no instructions from Jesus to abandon the Jewish dietary laws (e.g. the prohibition against pork). Peter, for example, is represented as saying, 'I have never eaten anything that is common or unclean' (Acts 10.14). The sentence, 'Thus he declared all foods clean' (Mark 7.20), is, as scholars agree, a late addition to the Gospel. Jesus might disagree with rabbinic health precautions, but he certainly did not wish to deny the validity of dietary laws plainly stated in Scripture.

Washing the inside

Even less likely is the possibility of a reference to ritual-purity laws in Jesus' saying, 'Clean the inside of the cup first; then the outside will be clean also' (Matthew 23.26). Some scholars have thought that this refers to some curious Pharisee law by which cups were ritually washed on the outside, but not on the inside; but there is no such law. The simplest explanation of Jesus' saying is the best: that he was talking about clean and dirty cups in the ordinary sense (not in the sense of ritual defilement) as a metaphor for clean and dirty personalities, both cups and personalities having an outer and an inner aspect. The saying was directed against hypocrites, who present a spotless appearance on the outsie, while being corrupt within. Similarly, the rabbinic writings speak of a sincere person as one 'whose inside is like his outside'. One rabbinic passage compares a hypocrite to 'a white pitcher full of ashes', which is similar to Jesus' picture of a cup dirty on the outside but clean on the inside, and also to his image of 'whited sepulchres'.

The Pharisees were much concerned about the phenomenon of hypocrisy, and many of their sayings are directed against it. An example is: 'Hypocrites wrap their prayer-shawls around them; they put phylacteries on their heads, and they oppress the poor. Of them it is written, "Behold the tears of the oppressed, and they have no comforter" (Ecclesiastes 4.1), and it is said, "Cursed be they who do the work of the Lord deceitfully" (Jeremiah 48.10)' (Ecclesiastes Rabbah, IV. 1.1). (Compare Matthew 23.5.) Jesus' sayings against hypocrisy are thus typical of Pharisee thinking, although, unfortunately, prejudice against the Pharisees caused a remodelling of Jesus' sayings by which they were directed primarily against Pharisees, not against hypocrites in general. The result has been a blackening of the Pharisees in Western culture, so that their name has become synonymous with 'hypocrite'.

An undoubted reference to ritual purity in the Gospels shows Jesus supporting it. When Jesus cured a leper, he told him, 'Shew thyself to the priest, and offer for thy cleansing those things which Moses commanded' (Mark 1.44; see also Matthew 8.4, Luke 5.14). Here Jesus gives his support to the ritual by which a leper, having been cured, achieved final purity (Leviticus 14.1–32). This passage shows Jesus as an observant Jew, concerned with the fulfilling of the Jewish law.

This is a case of biblical purity law (see Luke 2.22 for another instance, the purifying of Mary after the birth of Jesus). The practice of the *haberim*, or 'table-fellowships', however, was not based on any biblical law, but was in the nature of a voluntary vow. It is remarkable that despite attempts to explain the alleged hostility of the Pharisees to Jesus in terms of ritual purity, there is not one reference to the 'table-fellowships' in the New Testament. This shows that ritual purity was not the great issue in Jewish life that it has often been assumed to be. Even anti-Pharisee documents, such as the Gospels, although charging the Pharisees with hypocrisy, pride and over-meticulous attention to tithing, never accuse them of forming 'table-fellowships' from which ordinary people were excluded as 'sinners'. The picture of Pharisees cutting themselves off from the 'people of the land' because they regarded them with abhorrence as unclean, is based on a misconception of the role of ritual purity in Jewish life and in Pharisee thinking of the period. On the contrary, the evidence of both Josephus and of the New Testament (despite its frequent hostility) is that the Pharisees were loved and supported by the common people (for the New Testament, for example, see the description of Gamaliel as 'held in high regard by all the people', Acts 5.34; we know from the rabbinic literature that Gamaliel was not just a Pharisee, but the leader of the whole Pharisee party at this time). Ritual purity was not a matter that divided the Pharisees from the common people, who, as many rabbinic passages show, were trusted to be ritually clean at the proper times, and were not blamed in the least for being ritually unclean at other times.

9

The World-View of Judaism

Let us now consider the views that Pharisees shared with all other Jews of the first century—the views, indeed, by which first-century Judaism may be defined. These are that God had made a covenant with the people of Israel, and that this covenant took the form of a Law. It was the belief of all Jews that they were in a state of covenant (Hebrew, *berit*) with God, and that the practical operation of this covenant, on the human side, consisted of the observance of the Law contained in the Torah, comprising a way of life, the constitution of a state and a code of moral conduct. As long as a Jew accepted this Law, and made efforts to conform to it, however imperfect those efforts might be, he was in communion with God and a member of his covenant. If a Jew stumbled in his performance of his duties under the Law, this did not mean that he forfeited his position as a member of the covenant; for God had provided the means of atonement, by repentance, reparation and sacrifice, and by the observance of the Day of Atonement, and God was ever willing to forgive someone who turned to Him in repentance.

The Exodus story

How did this covenant come into being? Here we turn away from the formal conditions of being a Jew to the deeper dimension of myth. The word 'myth' is not used here in its ordinary use as meaning something untrue. As used by historians of religion, the word means a story, whether historically true or not, that has become the foundation of a religious culture. Every religion, ultimately, is based on a story: some saga of shattering events by which the world was changed. It is the imaginative impact of this central story that lies beneath all efforts of systematizing and theologizing. It is the story that gives the tone to the religion, and that provides renewal at times of tragedy and despair, when the original hopes with which the religion was founded seem doomed. Whether the story is based on actual historical events, or on the workings of the dream-world, or, as is more usual, on a combination of both, it rises to the status of myth when it informs and sets in motion a whole religious culture and acts as the imaginative background of the lives of its members.

In Judaism, this central myth is the story of the Exodus from Egypt. This is a story of release from slavery, and the values inherent in such a story have been basic to the Jewish religion ever since. It has meant that the Jewish concept of liberation or salvation has not been primarily that of release from some other-worldly evil or damnation, but from actual this-worldly oppression. It has meant that Judaism has always been a religion of this world, with a Utopian ideal of a world free of slavery and of the violence of the powerful towards the weak. Consequently, the liberation of the Israelites is accompanied inevitably by the concept of the Promised Land: that is, a land in which the slave-state of Egypt will be truly left behind because the liberated slaves, always mindful of the slavery they have escaped, will seek to set up a community of equality and justice and comradeship.

A third concept that is essential to this vision is also an integral part of the story: the crossing of the desert. For the Mosaic vision, unlike that of many other Utopians, was not a naive expectation of the speedy arrival of a perfect state of society. Instead, there was to be a long, hard struggle to implement the vision. There would be backslidings and rebellions, and only a long process of training and hardship would turn the erstwhile slaves into free people; for it is in the nature of humanity to yearn for the 'fleshpots of Egypt', and to wish to revert to childhood irresponsibility rather than cope with the hard tasks of adulthood. Entering into the Promised Land was not a happy ending, but only a beginning; the real Promised Land would be at the end of an even longer journey towards the messianic age, prefigured by short periods of partial attainment, such as the reigns of Solomon and of Hezekiah, and symbolically by the weekly celebration of the Sabbath.

Revolutionary ideology

The basic story of Judaism is thus one of political and economic liberation; in other words, of revolution. The only story comparable to it in the ancient world is that of the revolt of Spartacus, when a band of slave-gladiators broke their bonds and held the might of Rome at bay until they were eventually defeated. But the escape of the Israelite slaves from Egypt was a much greater event than the Spartacus revolt, because of its infinitely greater vision and idealism, and its determination to set against the political concepts of Egypt a new ideal of a human community, as would be set out in the Torah, and to implement this new ideal in an actual nation-state, carved out by force of arms and without compromise against the entrenched might of the military aristocracies of Canaan.

The concept of God implied by this story of liberation is also revolutionary. The divine symbols of the *status quo* are all swept away. The pagan gods, progenitors and supporters of earthly monarchies and aristocracies, are abolished. Instead there is one God, representing the central power of all Being; and every member of the covenant is directly in touch with this Power, without the mediation of privileged hierarchies, whether of kings, aristocrats, priests or gods. Even the *status quo* of nature itself is abolished: the sun, moon and stars are divested of divinity, and made mere creatures of a God who is above nature, and whose will can break through all cyclic regularities and rhythms. Thus man too is no longer subordinated to the rhythms of nature, but is lord over nature, which he can bend to his will and purposes—a concept essential to a revolutionary attitude, and to the Utopian ideal of a changed world. The transcendent God, mighty though he is, is interested in man's affairs on earth. The God of Israel has a far-reaching plan for mankind, covering the whole of human history, conceived not as a pattern of recurring cycles but as a story with a beginning, a middle and an end. He hears the cry of the oppressed, and makes a covenant with man by which he enters into a partnership with his chosen instrument, Israel, for the gradual development of the earth into a messianic kingdom. He will not be satisfied until humanity by its own efforts, but with his continual guidance, has turned this desert of a world into a garden, full of peace, knowledge, equality and justice.

This mighty revolutionary vision persisted among the Jews in all the troubles of their history, because it was inherent in the story that lies at the base of all Jewish thinking, that of the Exodus. When the vision seemed to be fading among the difficulties and temptations of ordinary living, there were always voices to recall it. The biblical prophets gave powerful expression to it, constantly reminding the people and their leaders of the basic symbols of Exodus, Desert and Promised Land. In first-century Judaism these symbols were as strong as ever, and underlay all the creative religious developments of the period, whether we consider the legal and moral structures of the Pharisees, or the dreaming of the apocalyptic sects.

There has been an unfortunate tendency, however, for some Christian scholars to see the biblical prophetic vision as continued only among the Jewish apocalyptists (see chapter 2) and not among the Pharisees, who are described as mere dry legalists. On the contrary, they were constantly invoking the Exodus symbols, even in their most precise legal discussions. For example, the second-century Abba Arika (a Babylonian teacher, known as Rab) argued the right of a worker to withhold his labour on the biblical principle that servitude to God means freedom from servitude to man, quoting, 'For they are my servants, whom I brought out of the land of Egypt' (Leviticus 35.42). Rabbi Eliezer (born about 60 C.E.), discussing whether a sword might be worn as an ornament on the Sabbath, replies that a sword is no ornament to a man, but an inglorious tool, since in the messianic age, all swords will be beaten into ploughshares. Discussing whether certain Sabbath laws apply only to the children of kings, Rabbi Simeon replies, 'All Israelites are the children of kings' (Mishnah, Shabbat 14.4). The ideals of equality and peace are never far from the surface, even in legal argumentation; or rather especially there, for the Law is the embodiment of these ideals. Indeed, if anything, the Pharisees were closer to the biblical prophets than were the apocalyptists, who had lost patience with the process of ordinary living, out of which legal discussion develops, and were relying on dreams of heaven-sent deliverance based on schematic timetables drawn from biblical texts. The Pharisees, like the prophets, did not 'separate themselves from the community' (as did, for example, the Qumran sect), but sought to influence everyday politics and to work within the community for a distant aim, combating the attempts of kings, aristocrats or priests to pervert the ideals of equality deriving from the Exodus revolution.

Life after death

On the question of an after-life, the Pharisees believed in 'the resurrection of the dead'. Both Josephus and the New Testament (Acts 23.8) attest to this belief of the Pharisees, but the rabbinic writings give us deeper information about it. Essentially, the Pharisee belief was in a bodily resurrection. All human beings (Jews and Gentiles) who had led deserving lives would come back to life, in health and bodily vigour, to share in the kingdom of God on earth in the last Days. This belief is found in the Bible, in the late book of Daniel in an explicit form: 'And many of them that sleep the dust of the earth shall awake, some to everlasting life, and some to shame and everlasting contempt' (Daniel 12.2).

The doctrine is also found in the Apocrypha in the Second Book of Maccabees, in the story of the martyrdom of the seven sons, who comfort themselves with the thought of resurrection. One of them puts it beyond doubt that a bodily resurrection was envisaged: '(He) stretched forth his hands courageously, and nobly said, From heaven I possess these; and for his laws' sake I contemn these; and from him I hope to receive these back again' (2 Maccabees 7.11). This was probably written by a Pharisee author at around 80 B.C.E. The same hope is found in the Psalms of Solomon (3.16), a Pharisee work of the middle of the first century B.C.E.; in the Parables of Enoch (chapter 51), written around the beginning of the first century C.E. possibly by a non-Pharisee author; frequently in the Testaments of the Twelve Patriarchs (pre-Christian, although subjected to Christian editing); in the Apocalypse of Moses (pre-Christian); and in 2 Baruch and 4 Ezra (both Jewish, about 70 C.E.).

The doctrine of bodily resurrection was thus well established. It can be traced with confidence to the period of the Hasmoneans, and possibly earlier. Its chief proponents were the Pharisees, although other sects too probably held it, and only the Sadducees definitely rejected it. It was a doctrine that fitted well the this-worldly emphasis of Judaism. Man had been ejected in the early days of the world from the earthly paradise of Eden; but in the Last Days Eden was to be recreated on a worldwide scale, and humanity would enter at last into the heritage God had originally intended for it.

It is especially noteworthy that this hope was not concerned only with individuals, but with humanity conceived in communal and historical terms. Individuals throughout history who had worked for this consummation of societal aims would be brought back to life to take part in it and to see, in compensation for their trials, a world transformed by justice and peace, flowering with all the best possibilities of human nature. Inherent in this vision is a faith in the ultimate goodness of humanity, and its capacity for mutual love and cooperation on a worldwide scale.

There was some doubt and vagueness, however, about the details of this vision of an earthly worldwide paradise. Would all human ills be abolished? In particular, would death? It is clear from some of the apocalyptic writings that some thought that those who were resurrected would live on earth for ever, as would those living at the time of the Last Days. Others, however (perhaps the majority), thought that people in the Last Days would be mortal, but would live long, healthy lives, as prophesied in Isaiah 65.20–22. Even the Messiah, the human king who would preside over the earthly paradise, would eventually die, and be succeeded by his son. This division of opinion reflects the varying answers given to the problem, 'Would Adam have lived for ever, if he had not sinned?' It would have been against the character of Judaism to lay down definitive answers to such questions. In theology, Judaism has always been a non-dogmatic religion, refusing to set up a hard-and-fast system to which everyone is obliged to subscribe. The Pharisees did insist on the doctrine of the resurrection of the dead as an essential belief, which they incorporated into the liturgy, but they did not develop the doctrine into an inflexible system.

In addition to the belief in an earthly paradise, in which the resurrected dead would share, there was also a belief held by most of the Jewish sects, including the Pharisees, in the immortality of the soul, although this was never formulated as a dogma. It was only a peripheral belief, not requiring urgent attention, because Judaism does not regard the soul as being in exile from its true home, to which it yearns to return. On the contrary, the soul has been given the task of cooperating with the body; only when this task has been successfully completed can the soul return to its origin in God, and this is regarded as a concept beyond the bounds of normal religious thinking. Thus the Talmud says, 'All the prophets prophesied only in respect of the messianic era; but as for the World to Come, "the eye hath not seen, O Lord, beside thee, what he hath prepared for him that waiteth for him" (Isaiah 64.4)' (b. Sanhedrin 99a). On this view, it was not the business of the biblical prophets to concern themselves with the immortality of the soul, but only with the fulfilment of human destiny on earth.

Nevertheless, the Talmud itself does contain some references to the ultimate bliss of the soul: 'In the World to Come there is neither eating nor drinking; no procreation of children or business transactions; no envy or hatred or rivalry; but the righteous sit enthroned, their crowns on their heads, and enjoy the lustre of the Presence of God' (b. Berakot 17a). The term 'World to Come' is often used to mean this condition of bodiless bliss, but it is not used entirely consistently, as it sometimes signifies the earthly age of messianic paradise.

In the New Testament, Paul asserts the doctrine of the resurrection of the dead, but in a sense that is foreign to the

113

traditional Jewish conception. 'Now this I say, brethren, that flesh and blood cannot inherit the kingdom of God; neither doth corruption inherit incorruption' (1 Corinthians 15.50). Paul therefore develops the idea of a 'spiritual body' with which the resurrected soul will be clothed. It seems too, from his account of this doctrine, that these spiritual bodies will not be situated on earth, the place of corruption, but in heaven. Yet the New Testament also contains traces of a more traditional Jewish doctrine of a messianic reign on earth (Revelation 20.4–5), and this remnant of Jewish doctrine inspired millennarian movements of social justice in the Christian middle ages.

The notions of a Day of Judgment and of Heaven and Hell belong to the sphere of the World to Come, not to that of the messianic age on earth, because they relate to the fate of the individual soul, rather than to that of the human race and its earthly destiny. The rabbinic writings, as well as the apocalyptic writings, do contain many remarks about the Day of Judgment, and about Heaven and Hell (*Gehenna*, or *Gehinnom*), but it is very hard to see any system in these ideas, and none of them have entered into any Jewish creed or even into the liturgy; for example, in the liturgy of the New Year and the Day of Atonement, the expression 'day of judgment' means the yearly judgment, not that at the end of the world. It seems that the most widespread conception was that *after* the end of the messianic age, when the story of mankind was over, there would be an individual reckoning in which all mankind would come before God for judgment; some would be appointed immediately for eternal bliss, and some for punishment. Some people thought that the desperately wicked would be utterly annihilated, others that their souls would suffer in Gehenna eternally. The moderately wicked, comprising the great bulk of humanity, would suffer purgatory (some thought for twelve months, others for only a few weeks), and would then enter a state of bliss. At this stage of history, it was thought by some, God would reduce the material world to chaos, and then perhaps create a new material universe in which a new story would begin.

These ideas, however, were held with such uncertainty and variation of opinion that they did not form the main focus of hope or fear. The average Jew was not affected in his daily religious life by a fear of hell. The rabbinic sermons, as preserved in the Midrashim, have very little to say about hell, and this was evidently not a subject of central importance in the Jewish consciousness. In certain apocalyptic sects, the topic was of more importance, but there was no Jewish sect that did not place the primary emphasis on the expectation of a this-worldly solution to the struggles of human history, in the form of a messianic reign over a world of peace, justice and prosperity, from which it was the punishment of the wicked to be excluded.

Who, then, were these wicked, who would be excluded from the messianic age? Some of the apocalyptic sects (for example, the Qumran sect) took a very narrow view. They thought that in the final great battles and cataclysms before the dawn of the messianic age most of mankind would be annihilated, and only a small 'remnant' (the term is derived from Scripture), comprising the sect itself and those who joined it in last-minute repentance, would survive. Among the Pharisees, there were some who shared this gloomy view, but most of them thought that most people would survive into the messianic age, where they would be joined by a vast multitude of both Jews and Gentiles who would be resurrected from previous ages. Here the Pharisees were following Scripture, which, though referring indeed to a 'remnant' of Israel (e.g. Jeremiah 23.3), also envisages a messianic age in which all nations of the earth will share (e.g. Isaiah 19.23–25, Zechariah 14.16).

God-fearers

Pharisaic Judaism, indeed, was a universal religion with a message for the whole of mankind. This was true, in fact, of every variety of Judaism; the only difference was that the narrower sects had lost hope that mankind as a whole would ever listen to the Jewish message. The universalism of first-century Judaism is an important historical fact that has some-how been overlooked. The New Testament itself bears witness that the Pharisees would 'compass sea and land to make one proselyte' (Matthew 23.15). Moreover, the Jews of Alexandria produced a considerable literature before and during the first century with the intention of winning converts to Judaism: into this category come many of the voluminous writings of Philo, Book 3 of the Sibylline Oracles, the Letter of Aristeas and others (see chapter 2). There is evidence from Roman authors that this campaign of conversion was very successful. Many Gentiles became converted to Judaism, and even more became what was called 'God-fearers', a category often mentioned in the New Testament, consisting of Gentiles who worshipped the One God of Judaism without becoming fully converted to Judaism.

This category of 'God-fearers' needs further explanation. Judaism has always accepted the possibility that people could be acceptable to God without being converted to its own system of worship, provided that they gave up idolatry and lived by rules of decent conduct. Thus in the first century, as in other centuries, Judaism, although adopting a conversionist posture, was prepared to accept degrees of conversion short of full acceptance of the Torah. This was a pluralist conception that took much of the urgency and hysteria out of the process of conversion. There was no hell-fire style of conversion-preaching, threatening damnation against those who did not become circumcised Jews. The reason for this was that Judaism was a universal religion, but not a universal church. Judaism regarded itself as just one way of worshipping the One God, not the only way. It was the religion of the Jews, who were a nation among the nations of the world, with a special pattern of their own, and their own special covenant with God. If a Gentile wished to become a Jew he was welcomed, but this meant not just conversion to a different religion, but also adoption of Jewish nationality. The Jews were regarded as a dedicated nation, the priest-nation of the world, and therefore to become a Jew meant to join a priesthood, not merely to adopt a new religion. This required a degree of dedication that could not be expected of every Gentile, any more than in Christianity every Catholic is expected to join the Catholic priesthood.

The God-fearers were regarded as having their own Patriarch, Noah, and their own covenant with God, which God made with Noah after the Flood. Noah, it should be remembered, was not a Jew. He lived long before the Israelite nation came into being. Yet he was regarded as a holy and good man, who worshipped the One God, and who received a revelation and covenant from him long before the covenants of Abraham and Sinai, a covenant not rendered obsolete by those later covenants with Israel. Any Gentile who subscribed to the covenant of Noah was thereby saved, just as much as a Jew subscribing to the covenants of Abraham and Sinai. The covenant with Noah involved not only the worship of God, but also adherence to a code of conduct which was known as 'the Seven Laws of the Sons of Noah'. The biblical basis of the Seven Laws was found in God's commands to Noah after the Flood (Genesis 9.1–17). It was held that the laws had been given previously to Adam (except the sixth, which did not apply to Adam, as meat-eating was altogether forbidden before the Flood). This code is found in various forms in the rabbinic writings. One form of this is found in the New

Testament, in the rules laid down by James, the leader of the Jerusalem church, for the guidance of God-fearers attached to the Jesus movement (Acts 15.20). The commonest version, however, is the following:

1. not to worship idols;
2. not to blaspheme the name of God;
3. not to shed blood;
4. not to rob;
5. not to engage in incestuous or other perverse sexual relationships;
6. not to eat a limb taken from a living animal;
7. to set up courts for the administration of justice.

(Tosefta, Abodah Zarah 8.4)

This code includes only one dietary law, which is clearly intended to prevent barbarous treatment of animals. This means that a son of Noah, unlike a Jew, is permitted to eat the flesh of all the animals prohibited as 'unclean' in the Torah. Similarly, all the ceremonial laws incumbent on a Jew (observance of Sabbaths and festivals, etc.) are not obligations for a God-fearing Gentile. This is an important point to grasp, because it is often thought that Jews regarded Gentiles as unclean and abominable because of their non-adherence to such laws. On the contrary, the Jews thought that Gentiles had the full permission of God to ignore the ceremonial laws, which formed part of the priestly code of Jews alone. The moral laws, on the other hand, as the above list shows, applied to Jews and Gentiles alike, and formed a *lex gentium* (literally, 'law of the nations'), or international law.

Sometimes, as Roman authors attest, a Gentile who had become a God-fearer would encourage his children to become full Jews. An interesting case in point is the royal house of Adiabene, who became converted first as God-fearers and later as full Jews. Adiabene, a client kingdom of the Parthian Empire, was the last remnant of the great Assyrian Empire which, 700 years before, overthrew and exiled the Northern Kingdom of Israel. By a strange twist of fate, in the first century (about 30 C.E.), this kingdom became converted to Judaism (see Josephus, *Antiquities* XX. 2.3–5 (34–53)) under its pious and devoted king Izates and his equally pious mother Queen Helena, who sent rich gifts to the Temple, as recorded in the Mishnah. Royal princes of this kingdom fought bravely on the Jewish side in the great war against Rome that resulted in the tragic destruction of the Temple.

Thus first-century Judaism was a universalist religion that did not seek to convert all mankind to its own particular pattern of worship, but envisaged a worldwide comity of nations, worshipping God in various ways within the broad outlines of the Seven Laws of the Sons of Noah. This concept was firmly based on the Bible. The book of Jonah, for example, portrays a Gentile city, Nineveh, which is brought to repentance by a (reluctant) Jewish emissary of the God of Israel; but the king and inhabitants of Nineveh are not portrayed as becoming Jews, but as becoming God-fearers outside the Jewish covenant. Similarly, in the visions of the Last Days of Isaiah and Zechariah, the Gentiles are portrayed as turning to the worship of God and reverence for his Temple in Jerusalem, without themselves becoming Jews.

Judaism thus made a clear distinction between the ceremonial laws, which belonged only to the priestly law of Israel, and the moral laws, which applied to the whole of mankind. Ethical monotheism was the creed that held together the whole of humanity.

10

Love of Neighbour

In the New Testament, Jesus engages in discussion with a Pharisee scribe as follows:

> And one of the scribes came, and having heard them reasoning together, and perceiving that he had answered them well, asked him, Which is the first commandment of all? And Jesus answered him, The first of all the commandments is, Hear, O Israel; the Lord our God is one Lord. And thou shalt love the Lord thy God with all thy heart, and with all thy soul, and with all thy mind, and with all thy strength: this is the first commandment. And the second is like, namely this, Thou shalt love thy neighbour as thyself. There is none other commandment greater than these. And the scribe said unto him, Well, Master, thou hast said the truth: for there is one God: and there is none other but he: And to love him with all the heart, and with all the understanding, and with all the soul, and with all the strength, and to love his neighbour as himself, is more than all whole burnt offerings and sacrifices. And when Jesus saw that he answered discreetly, he said unto him, Thou art not far from the kingdom of God.
>
> (Mark 12.28–34)

This discussion is very typical of the atmosphere of first-century Judaism. It is unfortunate that in the version of the above discussion found in the later Gospel of Matthew (Matthew 22.35–40), the atmosphere of friendly discussion between Jesus and the Pharisee scribe has been removed: the questioner is represented as being hostile, and Jesus' commendatory remarks at the end have been omitted—an example of the growing anti-Pharisaism of the Gospels.

It is quite wrong to think that the Pharisees were so occupied with minutiae of the Law that they never asked themselves what were the great principles on which the whole Law depended. Love of God and love of man were regarded as the two great pillars of Judaism. The centrality of love of God is shown by the fact that in the Pharisee liturgy the passage cited by Jesus, 'Hear

O Israel, the Lord our God is one Lord. And thou shalt love the Lord thy God with all thy heart and with all thy soul, and with all thy might' (Deuteronomy 6.4–5) was made the centre of the whole liturgy. Yet love of neighbour (see Leviticus 19.18) was regarded as even more central to Judaism, for it was singled out by Rabbi Akiba as 'the greatest principle in the Law' (Sifra 89b). Hillel, the great Pharisee contemporary of Jesus, when asked by a prospective proselyte to sum up the whole of Judaism, answered, 'What is hateful to you, do not to your fellow-creature' (b. Sabbath 31a). This is a version of the Golden Rule, which is attributed to many Gentile sages of the ancient world, and was also expressed by Jesus in the form, 'Therefore all things whatsoever ye would that men should do to you, do ye even so to them: for this is the law and the prophets' (Matthew 7.12, Luke 6.31). A negative version of the rule, similar to Hillel's, is found in the New Testament in Acts 15.20, in some texts. The trouble with the positive version, as Bernard Shaw pointed out, is that different people have different desires and tastes, so that my neighbour might not welcome receiving from me what I would like to receive from him! Note that Jesus adds, '. . . for this is the law and the prophets,' meaning that this is the essence of Scripture. Thus Jesus, like other Pharisee teachers of the period, was not announcing an independent moral principle, but commenting on the basic teaching of the Bible, which he too found not in the observance of ritual commands, but in love of neighbour.

The 'book of all humanity'

When Rabbi Akiba stated that the 'greatest principle' was 'Love thy neighbour as thyself,' another rabbi, Ben Azzai, disagreed with him, and said, 'The sentence, 'This is the book of the generations of man' (Genesis 5.1) is even greater' (Sifra 89b). This is a reminder that the Bible is the book of all humanity ('the generations of man'), not just of one people. Ben Azzai's comment points to a tension in Judaism, often misconstrued and simplified into the idea of 'Jewish particularism'. It is true that Jews felt a stronger bond and a deeper sense of obligation towards fellow-Jews than to humanity as a whole; but this was a matter of degree, not an absolute difference. In Judaism, there is a strong sense that 'charity begins at home', and that one's obligations towards family, friends and community take precedence over one's obligations to others. It was thought that there was something artificial about a charity that expended itself on unknown people far away, while one's own people were neglected (as was the case with Mrs. Jellyby, in Dickens' *Bleak House*, who was so concerned with the poor fan-makers and flower-girls of Borrioboolah Gha that she spent no time with her own children, and bundled into the street a beggar dying of starvation on her own doorstep).

This attitude is bound up with the Jewish type of conversionism, described in chapter 9. The Jews felt that they had been singled out by God, and rescued from slavery not to purvey to the world any brand of instant salvation, but to act as a kind of pilot scheme for humanity, in which, by struggle and slow effort, a society united by love, not power, would be built up. This revolutionary project was not easily exportable, if only because the Jews never felt quite confident enough that they had mastered the idea sufficiently themselves to act as teachers to humanity at large. Here we may sense a parallel with other revolutionary projects, such as the Russian Revolution, where it was debated between different factions whether communism should be promoted as a worldwide campaign or whether, on the contrary, efforts should be expended on 'building communism in one country'. Judaism, with its concept of the Promised Land, had chosen the latter kind of alternative, but always with the long-term hope that if success could be achieved in the Jewish community, this would prove a model for the whole world.

The term 'neighbour' is therefore explained in the rabbinic literature as meaning primarily one's neighbour in one's own community, but then, by extension, the rest of mankind. An illustration is the following passage from the Mishnah:

> One should not prevent the poor of the Gentiles from gathering Gleanings, the Forgotten Sheaf, and the Corner of the Field. This is because the ways of the Law are ways of peace (see Proverbs 3.17).
>
> (Mishnah, Gittin 5.8)

The Gleanings, the Forgotten Sheaf and the Corner of the Field were the rights of the poor, as laid down in Scripture. All these were to be left for the poor to gather when produce was harvested. (For the Gleanings, see Leviticus 19.9–10; for the Forgotten Sheaf, see Deuteronomy 24.19; and for the Corner of the Field, see Leviticus 19.9 and 23.22.) This poor-law, like British welfare-state provisions, was instituted for the benefit of inhabitants of the country, whether native-born or naturalized. There was thus no legal obligation to allow the poor-gifts to be gathered by non-Jewish poor people who happened to be living in, or passing through, the land. Yet, as in Britain, this law was not to be applied with rigid literalness, for there were considerations, other than the letter of the law, to be taken into account, especially natural humanity to fellow-humans, even if these were idolaters. So the non-Jewish poor were to be allowed to share in the poor-gifts allotted to the Jewish poor, for the sake of 'the ways of peace'. This does not mean just to avoid unpleasantness and ill-feeling (another expression would be used to mean this, namely, 'because of enmity', Hebrew, *mishum 'eybah*). It means, 'to promote the cause of peace even beyond the letter of the law'.

The Jewish laws expressing 'love of neighbour', therefore, should be regarded as similar to welfare-state laws aimed at reducing the suffering of the disadvantaged within the particular community of the Jewish nation and to promote comradeship and equality; but they have implications for the rest of humanity too, providing a model of how to live in community, for they were also extended, when opportunity offered, to people who were not members of the Jewish community.

Obligations between Jews

In general, the Jews were instructed to regard fellow-Jews not just as fellow-citizens, but as members of one family. Thus certain forms of behaviour are enjoined between Jews that go far beyond what can reasonably be required between fellow-citizens. For example, Jews are forbidden to exact interest when lending money to a fellow-Jew (Leviticus 25.36–7), a prohibition that receives detailed attention in the rabbinic writings. According to the Bible, however, interest might be charged on loans to non-Jews (Deuteronomy 23.20). This might be regarded as discrimination against the non-Jew, but only in the sense that a person may discriminate by not charging interest on a loan to a member of his own family while acknowledging that such behaviour, if generalized, would be highly unrealistic and would render commerce on any wide scale impossible. Charging interest was not regarded as an inherently sinful act (if so, all banks would have to be abolished), but as an act appropriate to business relations, not to inter-familial transactions, in which the forgoing of normal profits is to be expected. The ideal was that of a holy nation, behaving within their own society on a basis of love, not profit; but this ideal was acknowledged to be too rarefied to be made into a universal code. In practice, it proved too unrealistic even for unmodified practice within the Jewish nation.

The reforming enactments of the Pharisees, although in many respects reinforcing the ideals of the Bible, also modified them when they proved unrealistic. For example, the biblical institution of the remission of debts every seventh year (Deuteronomy 15.1–2) had to be partly rescinded when it was found to lead to a freezing of credit, in a society moving from agriculture to commerce. (See Mishnah, Sheviit 10.3–6, for Hillel's institution of the *prosbol*, a legal document by which a loan could be exempted from the law of the seventh-year cancellation of debts.) Even the prohibition against lending money on interest to fellow-Jews had to be modified in a business (not personal) context.

Thus it must be acknowledged that the high ideal of 'Love thy neighbour as thyself' was interpreted in first-century Judaism as largely applying to the relations between Jews, whereas a somewhat lower ideal was regarded as applying to relations between Jews and non-Jews—one arising from membership of the human race rather than membership of a closely-knit family, and requiring honourable and fair, rather than loving, conduct. It has often been asserted that this discrimination shows the inferiority of Jewish 'particularism' to Christian universalism, as expressed in Paul's dictum, 'There is neither Jew nor Greek, there is neither bond nor free, there is neither male nor female: for ye are all one in Christ Jesus' (Galatians 3.28).

It should be noted, however, that Paul does not say that there is no difference between being a Christian and being a non-Christian. On the contrary, his language concerning non-Christians is far from loving (see Romans 1.29–31). What he does say is that once non-Christians become Christians, no distinction is then made between Jew and Greek, between slaves and freemen, or between male and female. Exactly the same could be said of Judaism: for all converts to Judaism were regarded as on a par with born Jews and as sharing equally in the World to Come.

The alleged difference between Christianity and Judaism in respect of the definition of love of neighbour is often thought to be illustrated in Jesus' parable of the Good Samaritan (Luke 10.30–36). Jesus, it is argued, is extending the definition of 'neighbour' beyond the Jewish concept, to include the Samaritans, a sect held in abhorrence by the Jews; thence, by implication, he includes all humanity. The Samaritans (see chapter 2) were a sect of heretics whom the Pharisees at first classed as Jews. As late as the redaction of the Mishnah (200 C.E.), they were still regarded as Jews (see Mishnah, Berakot 7.1); after this time, however, they were classed as idolaters. The duties of love of neighbour, therefore, would certainly have extended to the Samaritans in

Jesus' time, despite the strained personal relations between the Samaritans and other Jews; for example, they were entitled, if poor, to collect the Gleanings, the Forgotten Sheaf, and the Corner of the Field by right (not just by virtue of the rabbinical ordinance which extended this right to non-Jews), and it was forbidden to exact interest from them. Certainly the Samaritans were regarded as heretics, and even feared because of their practice of waylaying and robbing pilgrims to Jerusalem.

However, the parable of the Good Samaritan is not about whether a Samaritan should be treated as a neighbour, but about a Samaritan who acted as a good neighbour to a Jew. It belongs to a well-known genre of Pharisee stories in which a good action of a Gentile idolator or a Jewish sinner is held up for admiration, the moral being that a noble deed should be taken as a model, however humble or sinful (in other respects) its performer. To this genre belongs the story of the Gentile idolater, Dama ben Netina, of Askelon, who won the admiration of the rabbis by his exemplary honouring of his father and mother (Palestinian Talmud, Peah 1.1); even the detail that he worshipped the stone on which his father, during his lifetime, had sat is told with approval because, although this was idol-worship, it evidenced praiseworthy honouring of his father. Another example of this genre is the story of Pentekaka (Palestinian Talmud, Taanit 1.4), so called because he committed five sins in relation to harlots every day. Yet because of one good deed (saving a woman from enforced harlotry), he was regarded as worthy to lead the congregation in prayers for rain. Further, the story of the Good Samaritan shows that since Jews of good standing, the priest and the Levite, failed to fulfil the commandment of love of neighbour, it is essential to look at the deed, not the person. Indeed, it seems probable that the story of the Good Samaritan was not a 'parable', but the narration of an actual event, like the stories cited above.

The story of the Good Samaritan thus does not step outside the limits of the religion of the Pharisees, but points a well-known Pharisee moral (see also chapter 8 for the alleged ritual-purity aspect of the story). Indeed, the first of the two Pharisee stories cited above goes even beyond the story of the Good Samaritan, since it calls for admiration for a practising idolater, not merely for a Samaritan, who was after all a monotheist.

It is certainly an important aspect of universalism to recognize a good deed even when performed by a heretic or an idolater, and to condemn a bad deed even when performed by an ahherent of what one regards as the true faith. Both Jesus and the Pharisees, through this genre of stories, did just this. But there is no implication that heresy or idolatry are to be regarded as just as good as Judaism. To commend a good deed by a Samaritan is not to say that Samaritanism is an acceptable belief. Jesus, indeed, according to the Gospel of John, condemned Samaritanism as a doctrine, and there is no contradiction between this condemnation and his praise of the Good Samaritan.

Very much in accordance with Jesus' commendation of the Good Samaritan is the following statement of the rabbis about the Samaritans: 'Every commandment which the Samaritans accept as God-given, they observe with greater conscientiousness than Israel' (b. Hullin 4a, Tosefta Pesahim 2.15, and elsewhere). The Samaritans are regarded as heretics because of their selectiveness in the acceptance of commandments, but they are commended for their zealous observance of the commandments in which they believe.

Inequalities in society

The above discussion shows that the Jewish concept of love of neighbour, although containing some gradation, was not in contradiction with principles of universalism. We may now enquire into certain problematic areas in Jewish institutions which seem not to be in accordance with the principle of equality. These concern the existence of slavery, and the disabilities of the *mamzerim* (bastards).

Certainly, love of neighbour demands equality and the abolition of class distinctions, and it cannot be said that Jewish society of the first century was entirely devoid of such distinctions. It should be remembered, however, that the Pharisee movement was a reforming movement which was continually making adjustments in Judaism in the direction of greater equality, and it is not surprising that Jewish society was still in a state of transition towards the ideal. After all, Western society of the present day still has far to go to attain true equality.

1. Slavery

The Bible abolishes slavery of Jews to Jews. It allows, however, a Jew to become a bondsman for a period of seven years, after which he must be released, unless he voluntarily chooses life-long bondsmanship (see Exodus 21.1–6, Leviticus 25.39–43, Deuteronomy 15.12–18). This limited form of slavery was allowed to cover a case of bankruptcy so that, by selling himself, a person could pay his debts and achieve a kind of livelihood. The evidence seems to be, however, that this form of Jewish 'slavery' no longer existed in the first century. The Pharisees had made the duties and liabilities of the master of a 'Hebrew slave' so onerous that, as the Talmud says, to own one could cause one's financial ruin. The spirit of the Bible's injunction, 'For they are my servants, which I brought forth out of the land of Egypt: they shall not be sold as slaves', was at last taken fully to heart (although in earlier times it had been neglected, see Jeremiah 34.12–22), and the slavery of Jews by Jews had become unthinkable, even in an attenuated form. Further, the duty of redeeming Jewish captives from slavery to Gentile masters (Leviticus 25.47–49) was taken very seriously in every form of Judaism, so that no Jew was left long in captivity or slavery, a fact noted also by Gentile authors. To be a Jew was synonymous with being a free person. Here is a case where the gradualist approach of the Bible towards the abolition of slavery is seen to have borne fruit.

On the other hand, ownership of Gentile slaves by Jews was still permitted, in accordance with the biblical permission (Leviticus 25.44–46). The institution of slavery was universal in the ancient world, and it was impossible to abolish it altogether, although it could at least be abolished between members of the people of God. But here also reforms were introduced and biblical principles were applied, to make the position of even Gentile slaves much better than that of slaves elsewhere in the Greco-Roman world—so much so that it is doubtful whether even Gentile slaves in Jewish hands should rightly be called slaves at all. Firstly, by biblical law, in the Ten Commandments themselves, all slaves, whether 'Hebrew' or 'Canaanite' had the right to rest on the Sabbath day (Exodus 20.10), a privilege unheard-of elsewhere. Also, biblical law demanded that slaves should be treated as human beings, not as mere property: a master had no right to kill a slave and was executed for murder if he did so (Exodus 21.20, as interpreted in Pharisee law); in addition, if his master injured him, he was entitled to immediate freedom, even for the loss of a tooth (Exodus 21.26–27). Further, by Pharisee law, a Gentile slave had to be converted to Judaism; if he refused this, he had to be sold elsewhere. Once converted, he had the status of a Jew and was subject to all the Jewish laws except those from which women were exempt; this meant that in addition to freedom from work on the Sabbath by biblical law, he was also free from work on all Jewish festival-days by Pharisee law. As a Jewish 'Canaanite' slave, he was subject to certain disabilities: he was not allowed to marry a free Jew, but only another slave or a member of the low caste of mamzerim (see below). But his master was entitled to give him freedom at any time, without requiring any official authorization, and he himself could buy his freedom if money became available to him (as it often did); he then became a full Jew without any disabilities at all. The rabbis encouraged masters to give slaves their freedom as a meritorious act, and consequently the class of freedmen became ever larger, and that of slaves smaller (though in the Dark Ages, when the slave trade in Eastern Europeans developed into a major industry for Christians, Muslims and Jews, this position changed for a while; this, however, was long after our period).

2. Mamzerim

The nearest equivalent to the term *mamzer* (plural, *mamzerim*) in English is 'bastard', but this translation is misleading, for a *mamzer* means the offspring of an adulterous or incestuous union, *not* (as in English) the child of an unmarried couple; the latter in Jewish law suffered no disabilities at all. This reflects the fact that extramarital sex, where both parties were unmarried, or even when only the woman was unmarried, although frowned on as unseemly, was not regarded as a serious crime. Since the Hebrew Bible allows polygamy, even though in practice this was unusual in our period, a married man did not commit adultery by having sexual relations with an unmarried woman.

Adultery, i.e. where the woman was married to another man, and incest were regarded with great horror, since the Bible treats them as capital crimes. A *mamzer*, defined as the offspring of these abhorrent unions, was forbidden by biblical law to 'enter into the congregation of the Lord' (Deuteronomy 23.2). This does not mean that a *mamzer* was excluded from the Jewish people. On the contrary, he was regarded as a Jew in every sense, including 'having a share in the World to Come'. The meaning of the commandment, 'A *mamzer* shall not enter into the congregation of the Lord' was held to be that he must not marry any Jew of good standing; i.e. he might marry only another *mamzer* or a 'Canaanite' slave.

The result of this was a kind of rudimentary caste system, in that *mamzerim* were not allowed to intermarry with other Jews. It was *not* a caste system in the sense that *mamzerim* were confined to menial tasks, like the Untouchables of India, but they were inevitably despised. A 'Canaanite' slave also belonged to a lowly caste, forbidden to marry free Jews, but his condition was not so desperate as that of the *mamzer*, as he always had the prospect of being freed, and so becoming a full Jew, whereas a *mamzer* had no prospect of release.

This was a situation which caused the Pharisee rabbis great concern, as they acknowledged freely that it was unjust to punish a *mamzer* for the sin of his parents, yet it was hard to see how an explicit biblical precept could be avoided. One rabbi declared that the tears of the *mamzerim* would be wiped away one day, and God would abolish the category of *mamzer* in the World to Come. Another rabbi pointed out that a *mamzer* could at least ensure that his children were not *mamzerim*: if he took care to marry a female 'Canaanite' slave, rather than another *mamzer*, his children would be 'Canaanite' slaves, not *mamzerim* (since descent in this case followed the mother), and they could then be freed and become full Jews. This rabbi recommended that this procedure should be followed as a general policy, in order to reduce drastically the category of *mamzerim*. Another rabbi, Abba Arika (known as Rav), adopted an even bolder strategy: he declared that God ensures that all *mamzerim* die young; thus there *are* no adult *mamzerim*, and the problem of intermarriage disappears. Unfortunately, this strategy was too bold for the other rabbis, who preferred to interpret Rav's dictum in a weaker sense—that all *undetected mamzerim* die young. This interpretation did indeed ensure that there were never any witch-hunts for *mamzerim*, since any cases of doubt were always treated as legitimate, and in this way, many *mamzerim* must have found their way to legitimation. But the problem of the undoubted *mamzerim* remained unsolved—a blemish in the reforming record of the Pharisees. This is particularly regrettable in that the rabbis *did* find a way to avoid other rather similar biblical bans on intermarriage within the Jewish community: the ban on intermarriage between Ammonite and Moabite converts and full Jews (Deuteronomy 23.3) was abolished by the ingenious legal argument of Rabbi Joshua (see chapter 4). It should be noted that there was never any problem about intermarriage between the priests (the descendants of Aaron) and non-priestly Jews (called Israelites). Such marriages were perfectly legitimate, the children taking the status of the father.

Thus Jewish religious society, despite its ideal of equality, had not yet attained this ideal in some areas. The drive to equality, however, can be seen in the reforming efforts made to improve the condition of the 'Canaanite slave' and that of the *mamzer*, imperfect though these efforts remained.

Welfare and charity

The great characteristic of Pharisee religion, however, was always its humanity. Even imperfect institutions were administered in a humane way. A saying of the rabbis is, 'This people (Israel) has three characteristics: they are compassionate, modest, and charitable' (b. Yebamot 79a). This saying is not a principle of general morality, like Hillel's Golden Rule, but an expression of the national ideal, the qualities that were to be cultivated as those of a true Jew. It contrasts strongly with the martial ideal of the Greeks and Romans. Mercy, effacement of self, and active sympathy were the most highly prized virtues.

These qualities are seen best in the great system of welfare and charity developed by the Pharisees. The biblical provisions for the poor, the Gleanings, the Forgotten Sheaf, the Corner of the Field and the Poor-tithe, were regarded as so important that it was laid down that any would-be convert to Judaism had to be taught these laws in his first instruction (b. Yebamot 47a). But these laws formed only a small part of the Pharisee system of charity for the needy. Every locality had its communal fund (known as the *quppah*, or 'basket') for giving a whole week's sustenance to the poor, a distribution being made every Friday. In addition, there was the 'charity-plate' (*tamhui*), which acted rather like a 'soup kitchen', providing daily distributions of food for the poor; this was available not just to the poor of the locality but also to the travelling poor, 'wherever they may come from'. These were all forms of public charity, but private charity was encouraged even more, since this could be given in secret in such a way that the self-respect of the poor could be protected. A person was expected to give one fifth of his income in charity; to give more was forbidden, since this would impoverish the giver and merely add one more to the number of the poor. A special chamber was set up in the Temple grounds where charitable gifts were put, so that people of previously wealthy background who had become impoverished, and whom shame might prevent from taking publicly administered charity, might come in secret to take what they needed. Charity was always to take into account the character and susceptibilities of the recipient.

In such provisions as these the Pharisees gave practical expression to the central principle of love of neighbour, which they regarded as the essence of Judaism.

11

After the Destruction

The Jewish War against Rome (66–70 C.E.) resulted in national disaster and also in great changes in the religious scene. The Temple was destroyed, and this was felt as a tragedy by all Jews (except the Samaritans, who had no reverence for the Jerusalem Temple). Those Jewish sects that had made the Temple the centre of their religious life, the Sadducees and the Qumran sect, were unable to survive the blow. Nothing more is heard of them after the destruction of the Temple.

Those sects that had staked all their hopes on apocalyptic visions also failed to survive the disaster for any long period. The Zealots, who had instigated the Jewish War, suffered great losses in their last-ditch resistance, but some survived, and continued to work for the overthrow of Rome, until more disasters under Trajan and finally under Hadrian (the Bar Kokhba revolt, 132–35 C.E.) put an end to the story of Zealotism. The other apocalyptic movements that had given rise to the pseudepigraphic literature faded from existence.

The Jewish Christians (Nazarenes) of the Jerusalem Church should also be included in an account of the post-Destruction history of first-century Jewish movements. According to a Church tradition, found in Eusebius and later in Epiphanius, the whole Nazarene community left Jerusalem before the Jewish War and went to Pella in Transjordania. That this story is merely a legend has been demonstrated by S. G. F. Brandon and Gerd Lüdemann. The Nazarenes actually stayed in Jerusalem and fought in its defence, suffering heavy losses. After the war, they were dispersed to Caesarea and other cities, including Alexandria. The role of the Jerusalem Church as the Mother Church had now ended, and Hellenistic Christianity now began to make great headway. When a Christian Church was reconstituted in Jerusalem in 136 C.E., its members were Gentiles (as Eusebius testifies), and its doctrines were those of Hellenistic Christianity. It attempted, however, to claim continuity with the early Jerusalem Church, and the Pella legend was developed to give colour to this claim, since some of the members of the new Church had come from Pella.

Fortunately, Pharisaism, the only Jewish movement that had mass support, was well equipped to survive the disaster. The Pharisees had never made the Temple the centre of their religious life, and had never regarded its priests as their spiritual guides. Their organization under the Sages, now called Rabbis, was unaffected by the fall of the Temple. They mourned the tragedy, and instituted a fast day on its anniversary, the Ninth of Ab. But they did not consider that the core of their religion had been touched, since oneness with God did not depend on sacrifices, but on repentance, good deeds, and the study of the Torah. Their leader in the years immediately following the Destruction was Johanan ben Zakkai, who set up his academy and Sanhedrin after the war in Jabneh. One of his pupils was Joshua ben Hanania of whom the following story has been preserved.

When the Temple was destroyed, ascetics increased in Israel, and they abstained from eating meat and drinking wine. Rabbi Joshua engaged them in discussion. He said to them: My sons, why do you abstain from eating meat? They replied: Shall we eat meat, which was offered every day continually on the altar, and now is abolished? He said to them: Why do you abstain from drinking wine? They replied: Shall we drink wine, which was offered as a libation on the altar, and is now abolished? He said to them: Should we also abstain from eating figs and grapes, because they used to bring them as First-fruits at Pentecost? Should we abstain from bread, because they used to bring the Two Loaves and the Shewbread? Should we abstain from drinking water, because they used to offer a water-libation on Tabernacles? They were silent. So he said to them: Not to mourn at all is impossible, for the decree has been decreed, but to mourn too much is also impossible. But thus the Sages have said: When a man plasters his house, let him leave a small portion unplastered as a remembrance of Jerusalem. Let a man prepare everything that is necessary for a meal, and then leave one small thing undone, as a remembrance of Jerusalem. Let a woman put on all her ornaments, and then leave aside one small thing, as a remembrance of Jerusalem. For it is said, 'If I forget thee, O Jerusalem, may my right hand forget its cunning' (Psalm 137.5).

(Tosefta, Sotah 15.11–13)

Judaism had to continue even under conditions of defeat and subservience to a foreign power, but it had to be remembered also that Judaism was never intended to be an other-worldly form of spirituality. It was rather the religion of a functioning nature and state with a capital city, Jerusalem, which was both a religious and political centre. A limited form of autonomy was eventually restored to the Jews of Palestine by the Roman Empire, under the Patriarchate, the descendants of Gamaliel. This Patriarchate lasted until 425 C.E. when a Christianized Empire decided to abolish it. But Judaism was never satisfied with such limited autonomy, much less with the condition of powerlessness, exile and suffering that succeeded it. In every Jewish prayer, morning, afternoon and evening, and in the ceremonies of Kiddush and Grace, the hope was expressed through the centuries of exile that the Jewish state would be restored.

In the remaining years of the first century, however, the concern was to build up a system that would weather the coming storms and ensure the survival of Pharisaic, now rabbinic, Judaism. In 80 C.E., Johanan ben Zakkai was succeeded as leader by Gamaliel II, the grandson of the great Gamaliel who dominated the religious scene in Temple times, and who protected the early Christian leaders Peter and his companions. Gamaliel II, head of the Sanhedrin of Jabneh, extended its authority once more over the Jews of the Diaspora, and restored unity to the shattered Jewish world. His somewhat imperious personality clashed at times with some of his great contemporaries, notably with Eliezer ben Hyrcanus and Joshua ben Hanania, but the peace-maker, the younger Akiba ben Joseph, destined to be the greatest of the rabbinic sages, helped to heal these rifts. In those years a beginning was made towards the compilation of traditions and their systematization. This activity culminated a century later in the composition of the Mishnah, the Tosefta and the Halakhic Midrashim, which became the foundation of the two Talmuds and of the vast body of Jewish medieval religious literature.

The Pharisees of the first century thus laid the foundation for the Judaism of the next two millennia, down to the present day. The religious rites that they created, the Kiddush, the Grace, the Sabbath candles and the liturgy, still shape the religious practices of Jews all over the world. Their hope of a better world, and their patience in coping with the world as it is, made Judaism into a religion capable of surviving through long years of persecution. Their intellectual vigour and joy in life ensured that Judaism would not merely survive, but would continually grow and develop, finding new ways, philosophical, mystical and moral, of interpreting the Hebrew Bible and the mission of Israel.

Bibliography

Translations and anthologies

H. Danby, *The Mishnah*, Oxford University Press 1933.

W. G. Braude, *Pesikta Rabbati*, 2 vols., Yale University Press 1968.

S. Singer, *The Authorized Daily Prayer Book*, Eyre & Spottiswoode 1918 and 1962.

C. G. Montefiore and H. Loewe, *A Rabbinic Anthology*, Meridian Books (New York) 1963.

Background reading

R. T. Herford. *The Pharisees*, George Allen & Unwin 1924.

M. Kadushin, *The Rabbinic Mind*, Blaisdell (New York) 1965.

Hyam Maccoby, *Revolution in Judaea*, Taplinger (New York) 1980.

Hyam Maccoby, *Early Rabbinic Writings*, Cambridge University Press 1988.

G. F. Moore, *Judaism in the First Centuries of the Christian Era*, 3 vols., Harvard University Press 1927–30.

James Parkes, *The Foundations of Judaism and Christianity*. Vallentine Mitchell (London) 1960.

James Parkes, *The Conflict of the Church and the Synagogue*, Soncino Press (London) 1934.

E. Rivkin, *The Hidden Revolution: the Pharisees' Search for the Kingdom Within*, Abingdon (Nashville) 1975.

E. P. Sanders, *Paul and Palestinian Judaism*, SCM Press 1977.

E. E. Urbach, *The Sages: their Concepts and Beliefs*, Magnes Press (Jerusalem) 1975.

G. Vermes, *The Dead Sea Scrolls: Qumran in Perspective*, Collins 1977.

Index